Macmillan English Quest 4

Welcome Back!
page 2

1 Web Quest — page 5

2 New York, New York! — page 12

3 Activity Camp — page 19

4 Town Fair — page 26

5 Art Gallery — page 33

6 What do you do? — page 40

7 The Castle — page 47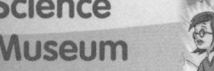

8 Science Museum — page 54

Mind Map — page 61

Cut-out Activities — page 65

Welcome Back!

Lesson 1

1. Read and match.

1. Hi, Anna. Good to see you again!
2. What do you want to do this year?
3. Hi! How are you, Olga?

a. I want to go on a quest again.
b. I'm great, thanks, Mr Fraser.
c. And you too, Charlie!

2. Look and write.

belt   tiger   mountain
gorilla
spaghetti
meatballs
palm tree
scarf
waterfall   sausages
boots
ice cream
cake
kangaroo
forest
chicken

wild animals ___tiger___
_____ _____

land features _____
_____ _____
_____

food _____ _____
_____ _____

clothes _____
_____ _____

Lesson 2

Welcome Back! 1

3. Remember the story: *The new classroom.* **Look and match. Number. Write the words.**

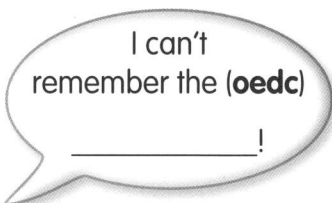
I can't remember the (**oedc**) _____!

Let me (**ese**) _____.

(**I – U – S – R – V**) _____.

Look at all the (**optrcmues**) <u>computers</u>.

4. Read. True ✓ or false ✗? Correct the false sentences.

❶ The classroom isn't new. ✗   <u>The classroom is new.</u>

❷ It has got computers. ☐   _____

❸ The code is 1-1-0-5. ☐   _____

❹ Mr Fraser can't remember the code. ☐   _____

❺ Victor Virus isn't using a computer. ☐   _____

Lesson 3

5. 🎧 **Write the months. Listen and check. Sing.**

~~February~~   June   April   November

January, (1) ___February___.
It's cold in winter.

March, (2) _____, May.
Then spring is here.

(3) _____, July and August.
It's hot in summer.

September, October, (4) _____.
Autumn leaves disappear.

Winter comes again in December.
Christmas and the end of the year.

6. Answer the questions.

❶ When is your birthday? In _____

❷ When is it hot? In _____

❸ When is Christmas? In _____

❹ When is it cold? In _____

Lesson 4

7. Ask your friends. Write their answers.

Name:	_____	_____	_____
What's your favourite sport?			
What's your favourite animal?			
What's your favourite food?			

Unit 1 Web Quest

Lesson 1

1. Look and write.

History   Art   Maths   ~~English~~   Spanish
~~I.C.T.~~   P.E.   Science   Geography   Music

Monday	Tuesday	Wednesday	Thursday	Friday

I've got English and I.C.T. on Monday.

_____ _____ _____ _____

2. Make sentences. Look and complete.

Olga	English	Geography	Science	Spanish
Monday	✓	✓	✗	✗

Charlie and Anna	Maths	I.C.T.	History	Music
Wednesday	✓	✗	✗	✓

❶ Charlie: What have you got on M__onday__?

Olga: I've got ___English___ and _____ on Monday. I haven't got _____ or _____.

❷ Olga: What have _____?

Charlie and Anna: We've _____ and _____. We haven't _____ _____ or _____.

5

Lesson 2

3. Remember the story: *The Quest begins again.* **Look and match. Number. Write the words.**

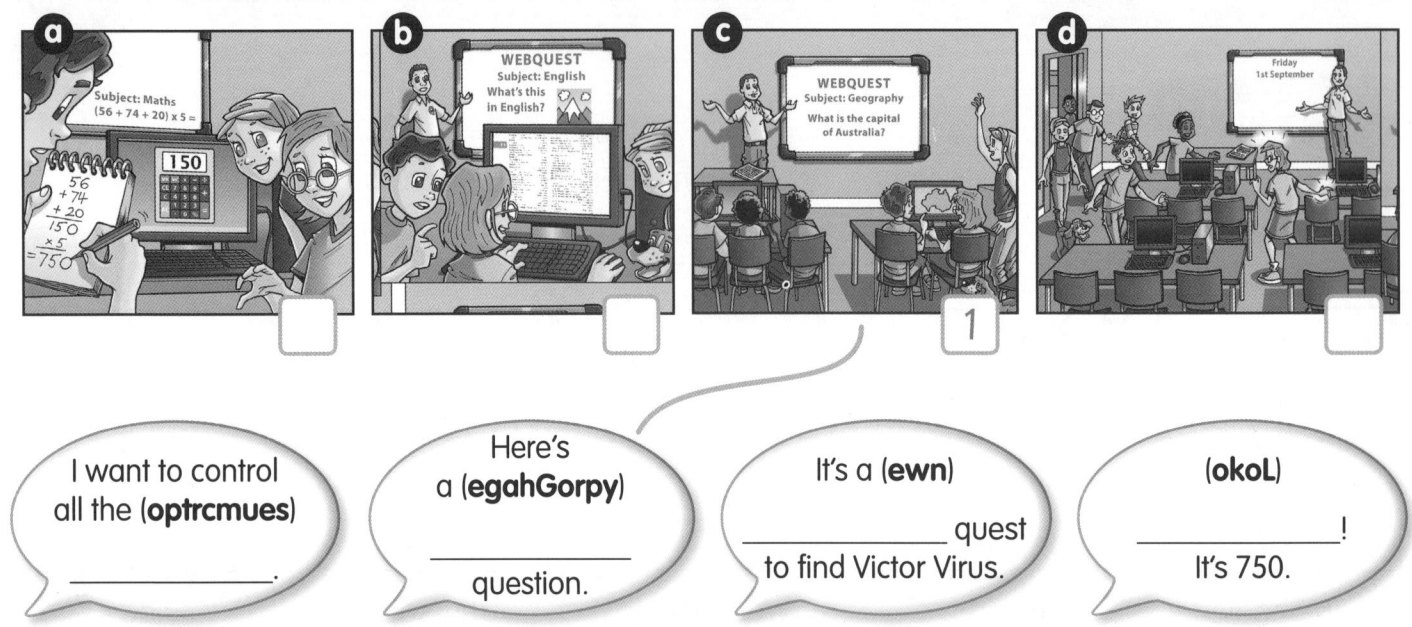

- I want to control all the (**optrcmues**) _____.
- Here's a (**egahGorpy**) _____ question.
- It's a (**ewn**) _____ quest to find Victor Virus.
- (**okoL**) _____! It's 750.

4. Read and circle the correct words.

1. The children work in groups of **four** / **three**.
2. The first question is a **Geography** / **History** question.
3. The children look in an online **dictionary** / **whiteboard**.
4. Charlie is **fast** / **slow** at Maths.
5. Victor Virus wants to control all the **computers** / **MP3 players** in the world.
6. The children have got a camera, **notebook** / **laptop** and bag.

5. Write the Quest letter. ___

6. 🎵 **Circle, sort and write. Listen and check.**

Geography fish dolphin afternoon photo Friday half

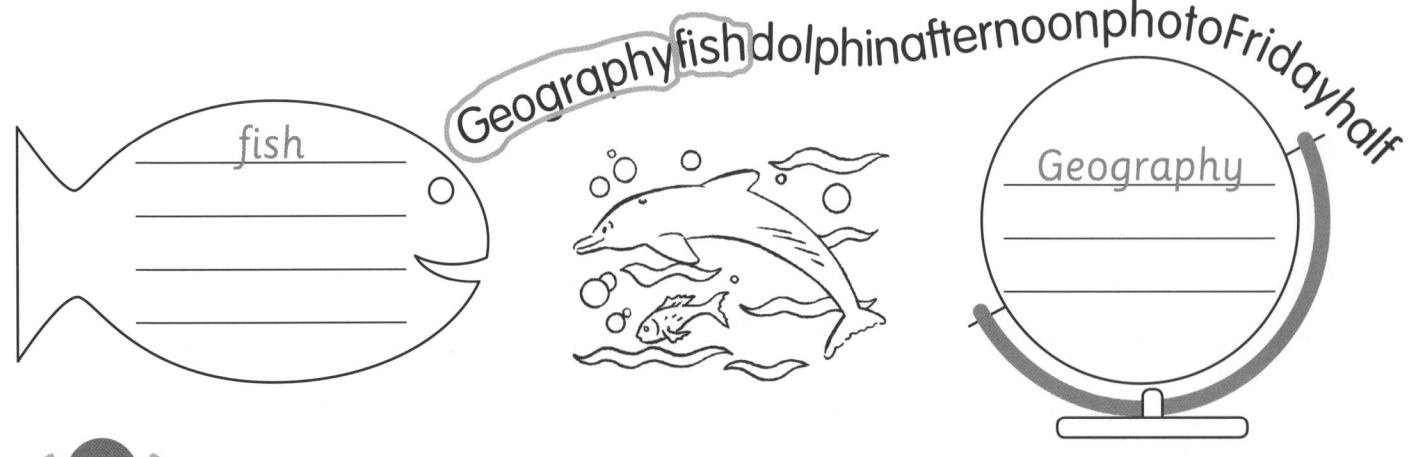

fish

Geography

6

Lesson 3 — **Let's investigate grammar!**

Web Quest 1

7. Write the words in order. Colour the boxes using the colour code from the Pupil's Book.

❶ got / Have / Spanish? / you

Have _____

❷ History? / you got / have / When

_____

❸ Maths / I've / got / at nine o'clock.

_____

❹ haven't got / I / Science.

_____

8. Listen. Draw the lines.

a 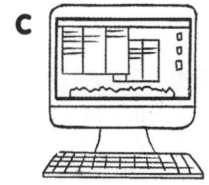   b    **Charlie**   **Olga**   g 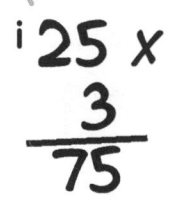   h

c    d HELLO!   e    f    i 25 × 3 / 75   i

9. Look at Activity 8. Complete the sentences about Charlie and Olga.

Charlie: I've got (1) ___Maths___ . I haven't (2) ___got Science___ .

I've (3) _____ and

I've (4) _____ .

I (5) _____ I.C.T.

Olga: I've (6) _____ .

(7) _____ . (8) _____ Art.

(9) _____ P.E. (10) _____

7

Lesson 4

10. Match to make sentences.

1. I've got — got Geography — have.
2. What — History — today?
3. Have you — I — Art?
4. Yes, — about — and I.C.T.

11. Look at Activity 10. Write the sentences in the dialogue. Listen and check.

Anna: Oh, Wednesday! (1) _I've got History and I.C.T_.

Olga: Me too! (2) _____?

Anna: No, I haven't. It's on Friday. Have you got Music?

Olga: (3) _____.

Anna: (4) _____?

Olga: No, I haven't got Art.

12. Draw and write about your school timetable.

Monday			
Tuesday			

It's _____.

I've got _____.

✂ **Do the activity on page 65.**

Lesson 5

Web Quest 1

13. Listen and number.

a    b  1   c    d

14. Look and complete.

| quarter to twelve | time | Music | it | half past ten | English | quarter past nine | Maths | How |

- (1) **time** — What ___ is it?
- It's (2) _____.
- It's (3) _____ class.
- It's (4) _____.
- Anna's in her (5) _____ class.
- (6) _____ do you know?
- What time is (7) _____?
- It's (8) _____.
- It's (9) _____ class.

15. Write and draw.

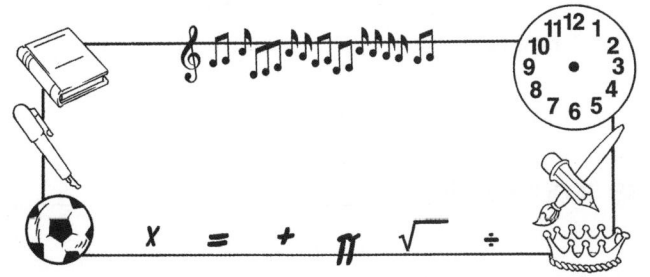

❶ I've got _____ at _____.   ❷ I've got _____ at _____.

Now do the Grammar section of your diary.

Lesson 6  CLIL Social Science

16. 🔊 **Look at page 10 in the Pupil's Book and circle. Listen and check.**

① In the UK, the school year starts in **(September)** / **October**.

② It finishes in **June** / **July**.

③ There are **three** / **two** half-term holidays, one in each term.

④ In Spain, the school year **starts** / **ends** in September.

⑤ There **are** / **aren't** summer holidays.

⑥ Some children finish at **five** / **seven** o'clock.

17. Read. Write about your school and stick a photo.

- in the USA
- August
- May

This is David in his school. He goes to school in the USA. His school is called Springfield Town School. His teacher is Mr Barnes. The school year starts in August. It finishes in May.
by Anna

Stick a photo.

I go to school in _____.

My school is called _____.

My teacher is _____.

The school year _____.

It _____.

by _____

Revision: Lessons 7 and 8

Web Quest 1

1. Listen and number.

 a  b  c  d

1

2. Read. True ✓ or false ✗ ?

❶ I've got Science at quarter to ten. ✓   ❹ I've got Music on Monday.

❷ I've got History on Thursday.   ❺ I've got I.C.T. at half past eleven.

❸ I've got English at quarter past three.   ❻ I haven't got P.E. on Tuesday.

3. Write sentences about your school timetable.

I've got English on Monday at ten o'clock.

_____

_____

_____

 Good    Very good    Excellent

Now do the Writing section of your diary.

Unit 2 New York, New York!

Lesson 1

1. Look and circle the correct words.

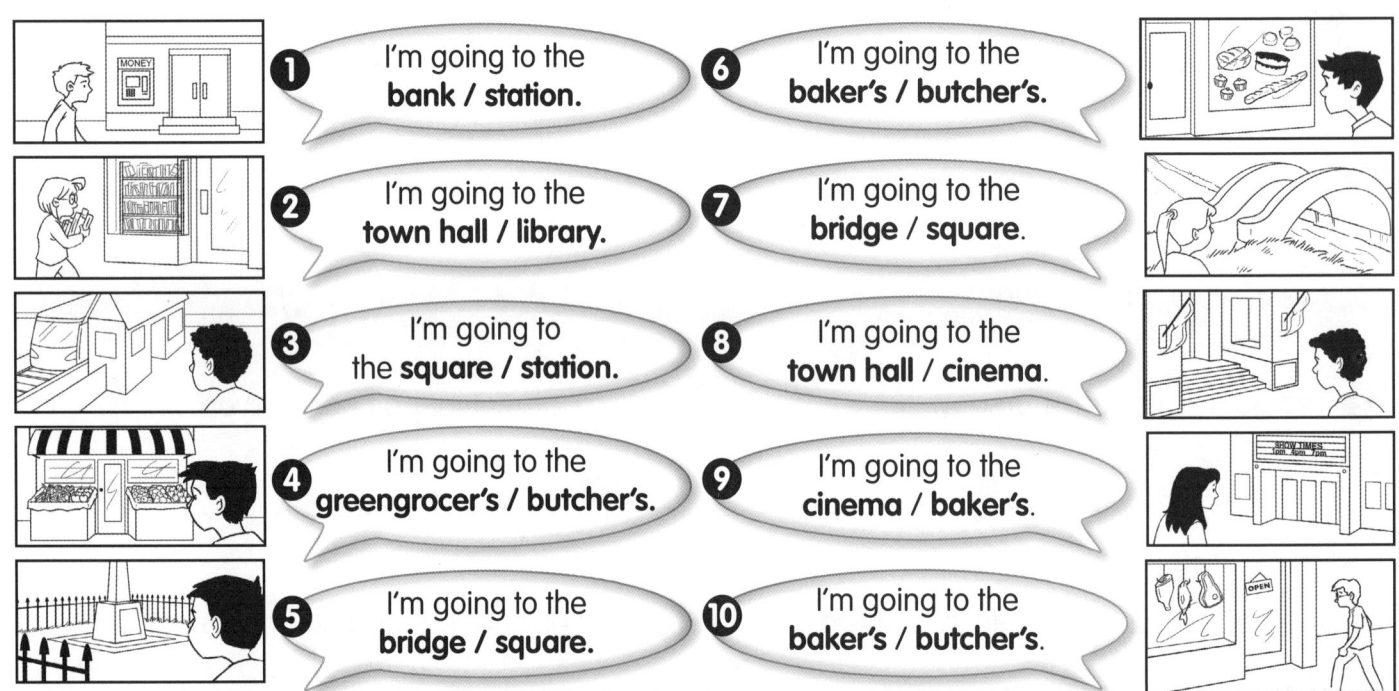

1. I'm going to the **bank / station**.
2. I'm going to the **town hall / library**.
3. I'm going to the **square / station**.
4. I'm going to the **greengrocer's / butcher's**.
5. I'm going to the **bridge / square**.
6. I'm going to the **baker's / butcher's**.
7. I'm going to the **bridge / square**.
8. I'm going to the **town hall / cinema**.
9. I'm going to the **cinema / baker's**.
10. I'm going to the **baker's / butcher's**.

2. Look at the picture and write sentences.

Where are you going, Charlie? I'm going to

❶ _the baker's_ and then ❷ _____.

Where are you going, Anna? I'm going to

❸ _____ and then ❹ _____.

Where are you going, Olga? I'm going to

❺ _____. Let's meet in

❻ _____.

Lesson 2 — **New York, New York! 2**

3. Remember the story: *A New York story.* **Look and match. Number. Write the words.**

a   b   c [1]   d

- That's Grand Central **(ttoSain)** _____ over there.
- I **(kihnt)** _____ it's Victor Virus.
- Victor Virus is in New **(okYr)** _York_ .
- Here are copies of the new **(optrcmue)** _____ game.

4. Read and complete the sentences.

> two o'clock   game   bus
> computer   cinema   ~~New York~~

1. The children are in _New York_ .
2. The children take the _____ to the launch of the new Quest computer game.
3. The Quest computer shop is between the bank and the _____ .
4. They go to the Quest computer shop at _____ .
5. Jim Jones is a _____ games designer.
6. Jim Jones gives the children copies of the new computer _____ .

5. Write the Quest letter. ___

✦ Phonics ✦

6. 🎵 **Circle, sort and write. Listen and check.**

bakerapplescakeatsandwicheslake

baker

apples

13

Lesson 3 Let's investigate grammar!

7. Write the words in order. Colour the boxes using the colour code from the Pupil's Book.

① the library? / you / Are / going to   Are _____

② the cinema. / I'm / going to   _____

③ going to / I'm / the station. / not   _____

④ you / are / Where / going?   _____

8. 🎧 Listen. Tick ✓ or cross ✗.

9. Look at Activity 8. Write sentences about Anna.

I'm going to the cinema. _____

_____

_____

Lesson 4

New York, New York! 2

10. Match to make sentences.

1. Where — are you — going?
2. I'm
3. No, — — not.
4. Are you

Middle column: I'm / are you / going / going to
Right column: the baker's. / to the butcher's? / not. / going?

11. Look at Activity 10. Write the sentences in the dialogue. Listen and check.

Charlie: Hi, Olga!
(1) _Where are you going_ ?

Olga: I'm going to the bank. Are you going to the greengrocer's?

Charlie: (2) _____.

Olga: You've got a shopping list.
(3) _____?

Charlie: Yes, I am. And
(4) _____.

12. Look and write the sentences.

1. I'm going to _____.
2. _____
3. _____
4. _____

✂ **Do the activity on page 67.**

Lesson 5

13. Look and match.

a 　b 　c　d

❶ turn left　❷ walk around　❸ go straight on　❹ turn right

14. Look and complete.

Turn right　Walk around　~~turn left~~　baker's

How can I get to the station?

First, (1) _turn left_ at the bank. Go straight on. (2) _____ the square. (3) _____ at the (4) _____. The station is in front of the baker's.

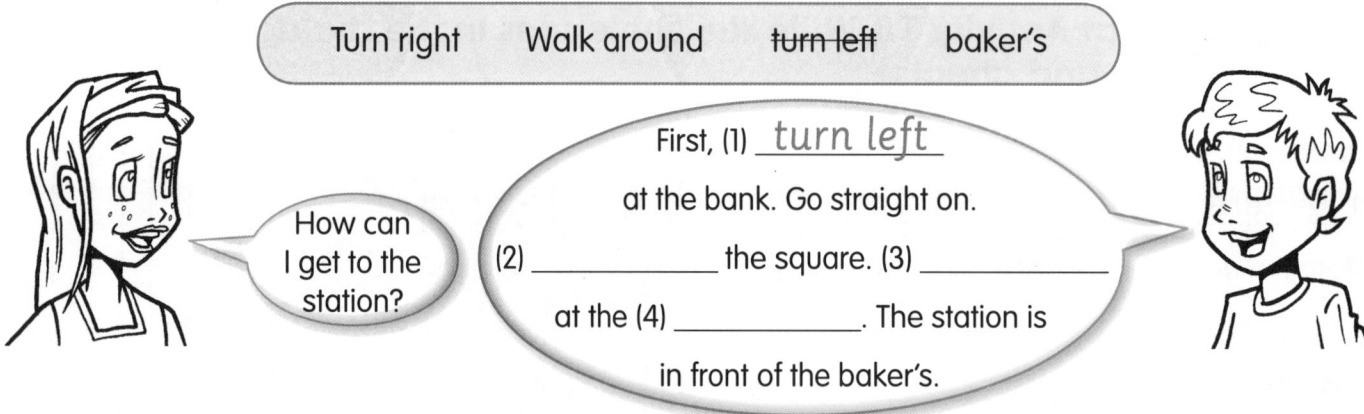

15. Look at the picture in Activity 14. Complete the sentences.

How (1) _____ greengrocer's?

First, (2) _____. (3) _____ . The greengrocer's is in front of (4) _____.

Now do the Grammar section of your diary.

Lesson 6

16. Read. True ✓ or false ✗ ?

1. London is the capital of England. ✓
2. There are 22 bridges across the Thames. ☐
3. Tower Bridge is a road bridge. ☐
4. Cars can go under Tower Bridge. ☐
5. The Houses of Parliament are where the UK Government meets. ☐
6. Big Ben is a clock tower. ☐

17. Read. Write about a city.

- Madrid in Spain
- a big city
- 128 neighbourhoods
- banks, cinemas, shops and stations

- Toronto in Canada
- a very big city
- a lake called Lake Ontario
- the CN Tower, cinemas, bridges and libraries

This is Madrid in Spain.
It is a big city.
It has got 128 neighbourhoods!
You can see banks, cinemas, shops and stations.
by Charlie

Revision: Lessons 7 and 8

1. Listen and draw.

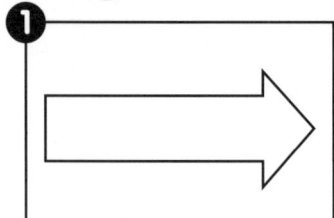
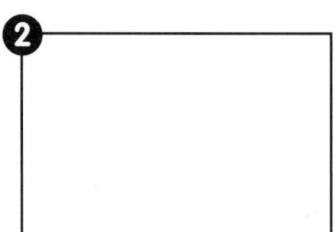
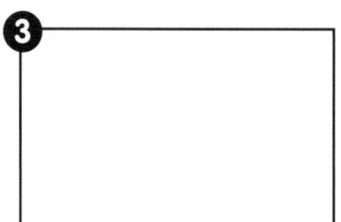

2. Read and match.

a

❶ I'm going to the station.

❷ I'm going to the butcher's.

❸ I'm going to the greengrocer's.

❹ I'm going to the bank.

❺ I'm going to the cinema.

❻ I'm going to the baker's.

d

b

e

c

f

3. Look and write.

❶ I'm going to the _____.
❷ _____
❸ _____
❹ _____
❺ _____

Good   Very good   Excellent

Now do the Writing section of your diary.

Unit 3 Activity Camp

Lesson 1

1. Read and match.

1. Olga is canoeing.
2. She's water-skiing.
3. Charlie is rafting.
4. Anna is cycling.
5. He's windsurfing.
6. He's camping.
7. She's swimming.
8. He's hiking.
9. She's horse-riding.
10. She's climbing.

2. Look and write.

What's everyone doing?

1. She's __horse-riding__.
2. He's _____.
3. He's _____.
4. _____
5. _____
6. _____
7. _____
8. _____
9. _____

Lesson 2

3. Remember the story: *The competition.* **Look and match. Number. Write the missing words.**

a — 1

This is a very high _____.

You're good at _swimming_.

You're _____ now.

That's _____!

4. Read. True ✓ or false ✗? Correct the false sentences.

1. The children are in the red team. ☐ _____
2. A boy is canoeing. ☐ _____
3. Anna is running. ☐ _____
4. The yellow team is good. ☐ _____
5. The horse-rider can swim. ☐ _____

5. Write the Quest letter. ___

6. 🎧 Circle, sort and write. Listen and check.

Colin

_____

_____

_____

c	o	r	b	x	h	c	e	l	i	a
l	c	c	o	s	p	o	o	t	m	h
i	y	e	d	c	l	n	o	l	i	l
m	c	f	a	n	t	a	s	t	i	c
b	l	d	g	c	a	n	l	m	a	n
i	i	u	s	l	c	k	s	f	l	t
n	n	i	n	i	s	a	u	r	i	g
g	g	y	m	n	a	s	t	i	c	s

Celia

_____

Lesson 3 — Let's investigate grammar!

Activity Camp 3

7. Write the words in order. Colour the boxes using the colour code from the Pupil's Book.

1. Is / windsurfing? / he
   Is _____

2. 's / swimming. / He
   _____

3. he / What's / doing?
   _____

4. isn't / He / canoeing.
   _____

8. Listen. Tick ✓ or cross ✗.

Is he/she ...	Charlie	Olga
swimming?	✓	
rafting?	✗	
water-skiing?		
hiking?		
cycling?		

9. Look at Activity 8. Write sentences about Charlie and Olga.

Charlie

1. He's swimming.
2. He isn't rafting.
3. _____
4. _____
5. _____

Olga

6. _____
7. _____
8. _____
9. _____
10. _____

Lesson 4

10. Match to make sentences.

1. What's — 's — isn't.
2. She — she — hiking?
3. Is — she — doing?
4. No, — Anna — climbing.

11. 🎧 **Look at Activity 10. Write the sentences in the dialogue. Listen and check.**

Olga: Look at the photos from the Activity Camp!
Charlie: They're great! (1) ___What's_____?
Olga: She's windsurfing. Here's another photo.
Charlie: Oh! I don't know. (2) _____?
Olga: No, she isn't. (3) _____. Here's another photo.
Charlie: Is she rafting?
Olga: (4) _____. She's canoeing.

12. Draw your friends and write sentences.

✂ **Do the activity on page 69.**

Lesson 5

Activity Camp 3

13. Listen and number.

14. Look and complete.

| can | ~~raining~~ | foggy | ~~canoeing~~ | swimming | hiking | can't | sunny | windy |

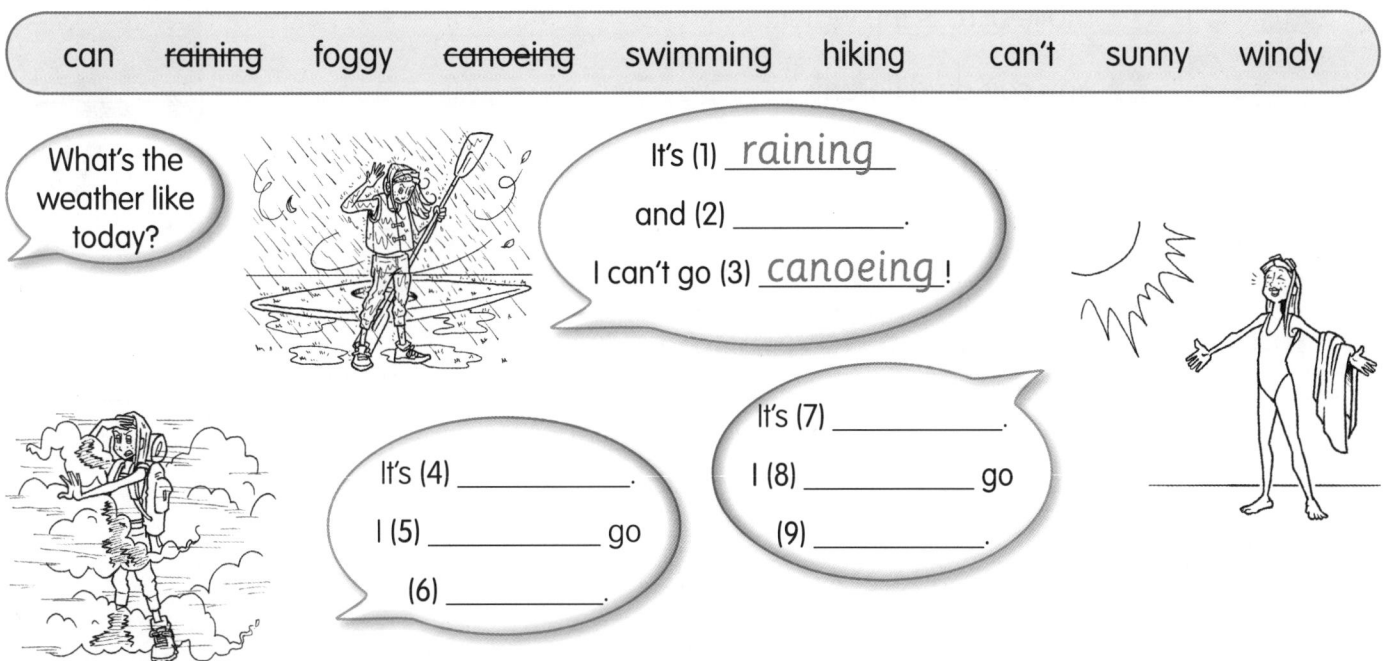

What's the weather like today?

It's (1) raining and (2) _____.
I can't go (3) canoeing!

It's (4) _____.
I (5) _____ go (6) _____.

It's (7) _____.
I (8) _____ go (9) _____.

15. Draw yourself and write.

Now do the Grammar section of your diary.

Lesson 6

16. Look at page 22 in the Pupil's Book and complete.

> a pulley   feet   the wind   boots   stunts   ~~adventure camps~~

❶ You can zip-line in forests, __adventure camps__ and river gorges.

❷ You use gravity, _____ and a line to travel from the top to the bottom.

❸ In kitesurfing, you use _____ to move across the water.

❹ You can do different _____.

❺ The snowboard has got special _____.

❻ You use your _____ for keeping your balance.

17. Read. Write about a fun adventure sport.

- mountain biking
- a summer outdoor activity
- a bike, a helmet
- ride bikes across hills and fields

- snorkelling
- a water activity
- mask, snorkel, fins
- swim under water
- see fish

Mountain biking is a summer outdoor activity. You need a bike and a helmet. You ride bikes across hills and fields.
by Olga

Revision: Lessons 7 and 8

Activity Camp 3

1. Write the words. Listen and check.

① It's (**ogfyg**) _foggy_ .

② It's (**nwnsoig**) _____ .

③ It's (**luycod**) _____ .

④ It's (**annriig**) _____ .

⑤ It's (**unsny**) _____ .

⑥ It's (**idwny**) _____ .

2. Look and read. True ✓ or false ✗?

① He's cycling. ✓
② She's horse-riding. ☐
③ He's water-skiing. ☐
④ She isn't climbing. ☐
⑤ He isn't camping. ☐
⑥ She's canoeing. ☐

3. Look and write affirmative or negative sentences.

① _She's camping._ ✓
② _He isn't_ _____ ✗
③ _____ ✓
④ _____ ✗
⑤ _____ ✗
⑥ _____ ✓

 Good

 Very good

 Excellent

Now do the Writing section of your diary.

Unit 4 Town Fair

Lesson 1

1. **Look and write the words.**

   ~~cheese~~   bread   sweets   jam   strawberries
   lemonade   pineapple   crisps   biscuits   pie

1. Can I have some _cheese_, please?
2. Can I have some _____, please?
3. Can I have some _____, please?
4. Can I have a _____, please?
5. Can I have some _____, please?
6. Can I have a _____, please?
7. Can I have some _____, please?
8. Can I have some _____, please?
9. Can I have some _____, please?
10. Can I have some _____, please?

2. **Look and complete the sentences.**

❶ Can I have some _cheese_, some _____ and some _____, please?

❷ _____
_____
_____

❸ _____
_____
_____

26

Lesson 2

Town Fair 4

3. **Remember the story:** *The cheese race.* **Look and match. Number. Write the missing words.**

Can I have some _____, please?

It's a big _____!

My cheese is too _____!

I love _____!

4. **Read and circle the correct words.**

The children go to a town (1) **fair** / **hall**. Charlie buys some cheese and enters a competition. Charlie's cheese is too (2) **fast** / **slow** and jumps the wall. Anna and (3) **Olga** / **Charlie** go to a fortune teller. The fortune teller can see a big (4) **cheese** / **pineapple** in the crystal ball. The cheese goes into the fortune teller's tent. Olga can see a Quest symbol in (5) **the cheese** / **the crystal ball**.

5. **Write the Quest letter.** ___

6. **Circle, sort and write. Listen and check.**

 bread

d	n	f	m	h	j	e	n	n	y
n	f	e	w	z	e	r	i	a	d
b	r	e	a	k	f	a	s	t	t
h	i	e	n	l	b	r	d	g	s
m	e	a	l	o	a	r	l	s	i
o	n	t	c	a	l	j	e	e	f
q	d	c	h	e	e	s	e	a	l
a	s	b	v	c	d	k	y	k	d

 cheese

Lesson 3 — Let's investigate grammar!

7. Write the words in order. Colour the boxes using the colour code from the Pupil's Book.

① some bread, please? / I / Can / have   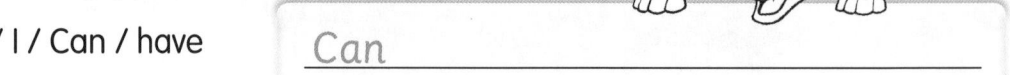 Can _____

② please. / five pounds, / That's

③ I / got / pineapples. / haven't

④ you / are. / Here

8. 🎧 CD2 10 Listen. Draw the lines.

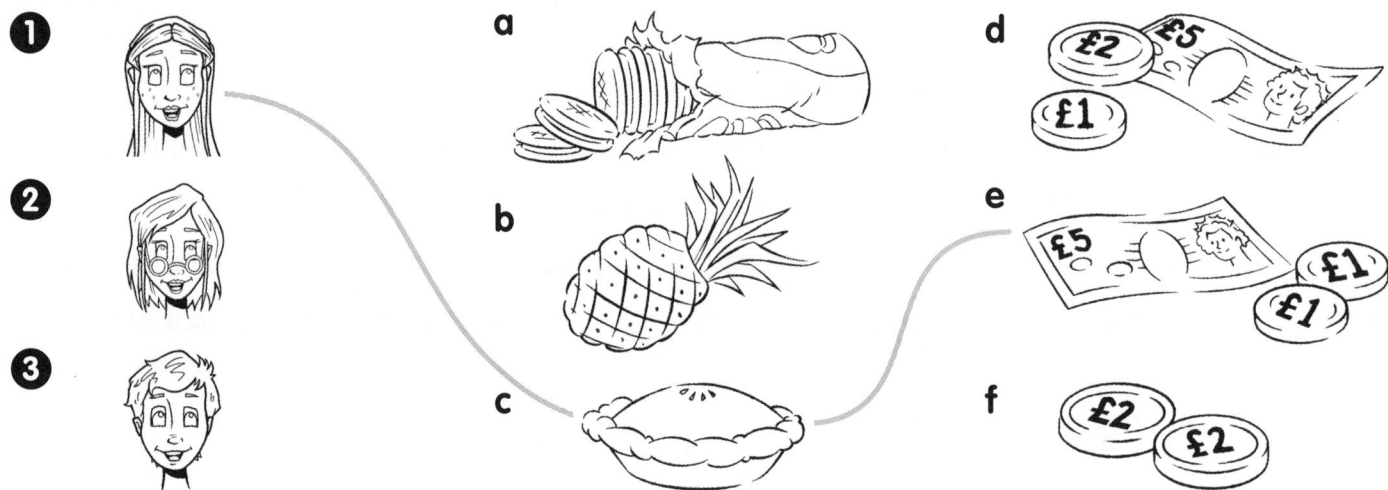

9. Look at Activity 8. Write the sentences.

① Olga: C_an_____ I h_ave_____ a p_____, p_____?

Charlie: Y_____, h_____ y_____ a_____.

That's s_____ p_____, p_____.

② Anna: _____?

Charlie: Yes, _____. _____.

③ Charlie: _____

Anna: _____

Lesson 4

10. Match to make sentences.

1. Can I have — some cheese, — please?
2. That's — four pounds, — ...
3. I — haven't got — ...
4. Here — you — are.

(matches shown: 1→some cheese→please?; 2→four pounds; 3→haven't got→pineapples; 4→you→are; please.)

11. Look at Activity 10. Write the sentences in the dialogue. Listen and check.

Anna: Hello! Can I help you?
Olga: Yes! (1) Can _____?
Anna: Yes, here you are.
Olga: Can I have a pineapple, please?
Anna: I'm sorry. (2) _____.
Olga: Ok. Can I have some strawberries, please?
Anna: Yes! (3) _____.
(4) _____.
Olga: Thank you. Goodbye!

12. Look and write the dialogue.

Assistant: Hello! Can I (1) _____?
Customer: Yes. (2) _____ some cheese, please?
Assistant: Yes, here (3) _____.
Customer: (4) _____ a pie, please?
Assistant: I'm sorry. (5) _____.
Customer: Ok. Can (6) _____ jam, please?
Assistant: Yes. Here (7) _____.
(8) _____ five pounds, please.
Customer: Thank you. Goodbye!

✂ **Do the activity on page 71.**

Lesson 5

13. Look and match.

a  b  c  d 20p e 50p

☐ ☐ ☐ 1 ☐

❶ twenty pence
❷ two pence
❸ twelve pounds ninety-nine
❹ fifty pence
❺ seven pounds fifty

14. Look and complete the sentences.

How much is it?

❶ It's <u>two pounds fifty</u>.
❷ It's _____.
❸ It's _____.
❹ It's _____.

15. Draw and write how much it is.

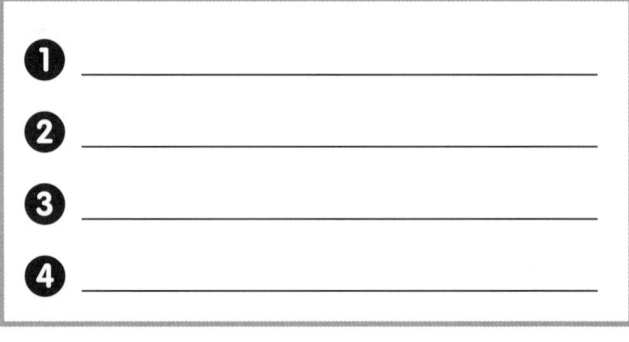

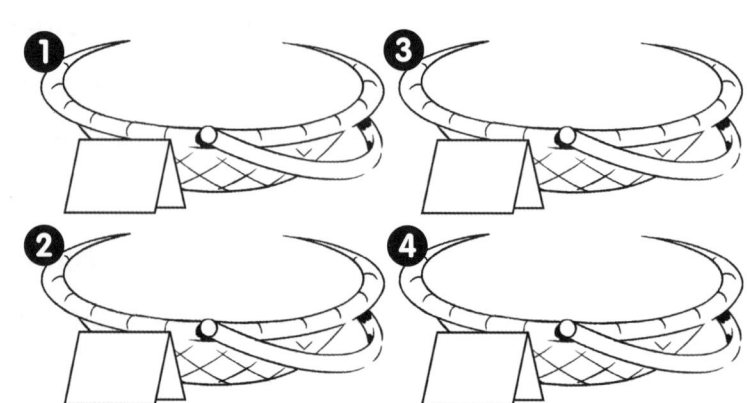

❶ _____
❷ _____
❸ _____
❹ _____

Now do the Grammar section of your diary.

Lesson 6

16. 🎧 **Look at page 30 in the Pupil's Book and circle. Listen and check.**

① The Euro is the currency in lots of countries in **Asia** / **Europe**.

② All Euro banknotes have got **the same** / **a different** design.

③ The **Pound** / **Dollar** is the currency in the UK.

④ On one side of the banknotes you can see a **dark** / **light** line.

⑤ American dollar notes are made from **linen and cotton** / **paper and cotton**.

⑥ The **one dollar** / **ten dollar** note has got a picture of George Washington.

17. Read. Write about a famous shop.

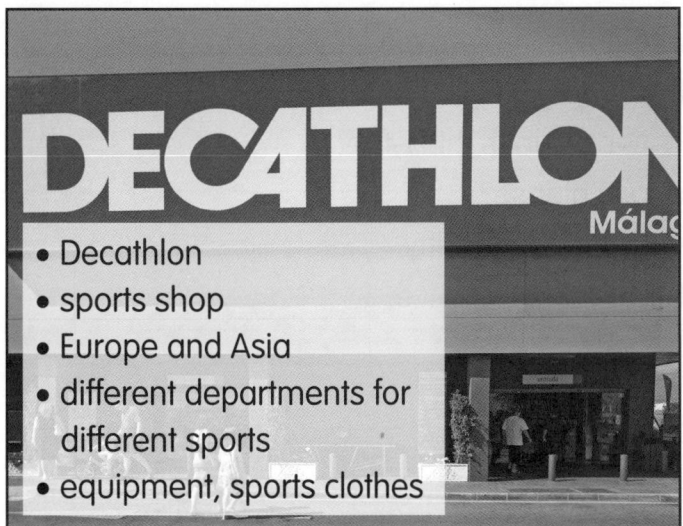

- Decathlon
- sports shop
- Europe and Asia
- different departments for different sports
- equipment, sports clothes

- Marks and Spencer
- department store
- the UK
- lots of departments
- clothes, food, furniture

<u>Decathlon is a famous sports shop in Europe and Asia. It's got different departments for different sports. You can buy equipment and sports clothes.
by Anna</u>

31

Revision: Lessons 7 and 8

1. 🎧 **Listen and number.**

a 50p ☐   b £7.25 ☐   c 15p [1]   d £14.99 ☐

2. Look and match.

1. Jam is — c two pounds thirty-five.
2. Crisps are — a eighty-five pence.
3. Can I have some — b cheese, please?
4. Sweets are — d pie, please?
5. Can I have a — e three pounds fifty.
6. A pineapple is — f ninety-nine pence.

3. Look and complete.

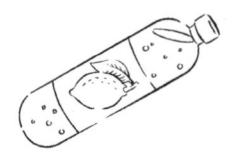   

1. Can I __have__ _____ ?   2. A pie is _____ .   3. _____ _____ ?   4. _____ _____

 Good    Very good   Excellent

Now do the Writing section of your diary.

Unit 5 Art Gallery

Lesson 1

1. Read and match.

1. She's got brown eyes.
2. He's got a beard.
3. He's got curly hair.
4. She's got long hair.
5. She's got straight hair.

a    b    c    d

6. She's got short hair.
7. He's got a moustache.
8. She's got fair hair.
9. She's got dark hair.
10. He's got glasses.

2. Look and write sentences.

straight	short
long	fair
dark	beard
brown	glasses
moustache	

1. Anna has got s_traight_ hair and g_____. She hasn't got a m_____.

2. Olga _____ _____. She hasn't _____ _____ eyes.

3. Charlie _____ _____. He _____ _____.

33

Lesson 2

3. Remember the story: *The thief in the gallery.* **Look and match. Number. Write the missing words.**

Can I look at your _____ ?

She's got __long__, straight hair!

And he's _____ the Mona Matilda!

I think the thief is in the gallery with the _____ painting!

4. Answer the questions.

1. Where are the children? ___at an art gallery___
2. What is the problem with the Mona Matilda? She's got _____.
3. What is on the floor? wet p_____
4. Where does it go to? into the s_____
5. Who finds the thief? _____
6. What does the real Mona Matilda look like? She's got _____.

5. Write the Quest letter. ___

Phonics

6. (CD2 27) **Circle, sort and write. Listen and check.**

___curls___
_____
_____

t	h	u	r	s	d	a	y	o	g	s
h	c	l	p	y	b	h	s	t	r	h
b	g	i	r	l	o	f	m	u	s	i
i	i	s	t	e	a	l	a	n	c	r
r	x	e	h	t	p	a	l	i	h	l
d	s	k	i	r	p	u	r	p	l	e
s	k	s	a	u	l	v	a	n	o	y
d	d	f	c	u	r	l	s	l	l	b
w	i	n	d	s	u	r	f	w	o	t

___girl___
_____
_____

34

Lesson 3 — Let's investigate grammar!

Art Gallery 5

7. Write the words in order. Colour the boxes using the colour code from the Pupil's Book.

1. curly hair? / she / Has / got — Has _____
2. hasn't got / blue eyes. / She _____
3. got / she / Has / long hair? _____
4. got / She's / brown hair. _____

8. Listen. Tick ✓ or cross ✗.

	Charlie's painting	Olga's painting
long hair	✓	
short hair		
dark hair		
fair hair		
straight hair		
curly hair		
It's number ...		

9. Look at Activity 8. Write about Charlie's and Olga's paintings.

Charlie
1. She's got long hair.
2. _____
3. _____

Olga
4. _____
5. _____
6. _____

Lesson 4

10. Match to make sentences.

1. Has
2. Yes,
3. He
4. He's

he
got
he got
hasn't got a

black hair.
glasses?
has.
moustache.

11. Look at Activity 10. Write the sentences in the dialogue. Listen and check.

Anna: Let's play 'Guess the painting'.

Charlie: Ok! Is it a girl?

Anna: No, it isn't.

Charlie: Ok! (1) _Has he_ _____?

Anna: No, he hasn't.

Charlie: Has he got straight hair?

Anna: (2) _____.

And (3) _____.

Charlie: Has he got long hair?

Anna: No, he hasn't. And (4) _____.

Charlie: Ok! It's this one!

12. Look at Activity 11. Look and write about painting c.

1. She _____.
2. _____
3. _____
4. _____
5. _____
6. _____

✂ **Do the activity on page 73.**

Lesson 5

13. Write the words.

❶ _happy_ ❷ _____ ❸ _____ ❹ _____ ❺ _____ ❻ _____

14. Look and read. Complete the sentences.

He's got short, curly hair. Which number is he?

Number __1__!
He's __happy__.

She's got long, dark hair. Which number is she?

Number ____!
She's _____.

He's got a moustache. He's got straight hair. Which number is he?

He's _____.

She's got straight, fair hair. Which number is she?

_____
_____

15. Draw a friend and write sentences.

This is _____.

_____
_____
_____

Now do the Grammar section of your diary.

Lesson 6

16. Read. True ✓ or false ✗ ?

1. This is a new painting by Diego Velázquez. ✗
2. This type of painting is called realism. ☐
3. Velázquez has got dark, curly hair. ☐
4. He's got a moustache. ☐
5. Princess Margarita has got curly, fair hair. ☐
6. María Agustina has got short, curly hair. ☐
7. She's offering some biscuits to the Princess. ☐

17. Read. Write about a child's painting.

- self portrait
- different shapes and colours
- long, black hair
- brown eyes

This is a self portrait.
The painter uses different shapes and colours.
The girl has got long, black hair and brown eyes.
by Charlie

- self portrait
- different shapes and colours
- short, black hair
- glasses

Revision: Lessons 7 and 8

Art Gallery 5

1. **Match. Listen and check.**

a He's rude.

 ①  ②  ③

d She's sad.

b He's strong.

 ④  ⑤  ⑥

e She's weak.

c He's happy.

f She's polite.

2. **Read. True ✓ or false ✗ ?**

① He's got curly hair. ☐
② He hasn't got long hair. ☐
③ He hasn't got dark hair. ☐
④ He's got a moustache and beard. ☐

⑤ She's got dark hair. ☐
⑥ She's got long hair. ☐
⑦ She hasn't got curly hair. ☐
⑧ She's got glasses. ☐

3. **Look and write about Charlie.**

 Good    Very good    Excellent

Now do the Writing section of your diary.

Unit 6 What do you do?

Lesson 1

1. Look and circle the correct words.

1. She (leaves home) / comes back home.
2. She goes to a friend's house / goes to school.
3. She comes back home / leaves home.
4. She goes for a walk / meets a friend.
5. He goes to a friend's house / goes for a walk.
6. He has a snack / talks on the phone.
7. He goes for a walk / goes to school.
8. He comes back home / has a snack.

2. Look and complete the sentences about Anna.

~~talks on the phone~~   goes to   leaves home   goes for   has a snack

1. Anna _talks on the phone_.
2. She _____ a walk.
3. She _____.
4. She _____.
5. She _____ her friend's house.

Lesson 2

What do you do? 6

3. **Remember the story:** *The quiz show.* **Look and match. Number. Complete the sentences.**

Put on your _____, boots and _____.

Welcome _____ our fire _____!

We _____ catch _____!

She leaves _home_ at seven _____.

4. **Answer the questions.**

   ❶ Who is a contestant on the quiz show? _____Charlie_____

   ❷ What is his prize? to be a f_____ for a day with his f_____

   ❸ What clothes do firefighters wear? _____

   ❹ Where is Max? _____

   ❺ Is he happy? _____

5. **Write the Quest letter.** ___

✨ **Phonics** ✨

6. 🎵 **Circle, sort and write. Listen and check.**

dog   _bone_

_____   _____

_____   _____

Lesson 3 — Let's investigate grammar!

7. Write the words in order. Colour the boxes using the colour code from the Pupil's Book.

❶ he / on the phone? / Does / talk

Does _____

❷ friends. / He / meets

_____

❸ have / He / a snack. / doesn't

_____

❹ he / doesn't. / No,

_____

8. 🎧 Listen. Tick ✓ or cross ✗.

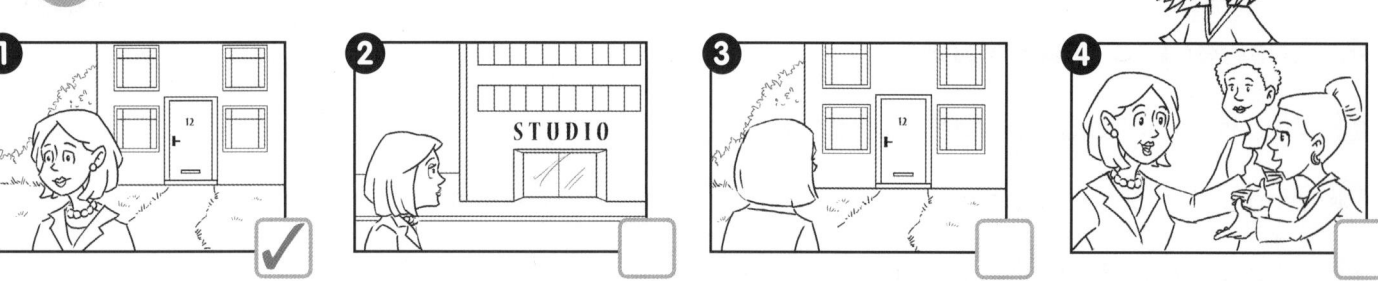

9. Look at Activity 8. Write sentences.

❶ She leaves home.
❷ _____
❸ _____
❹ _____
❺ _____
❻ _____
❼ _____

Lesson 4

What do you do? 6

10. Match to make sentences.

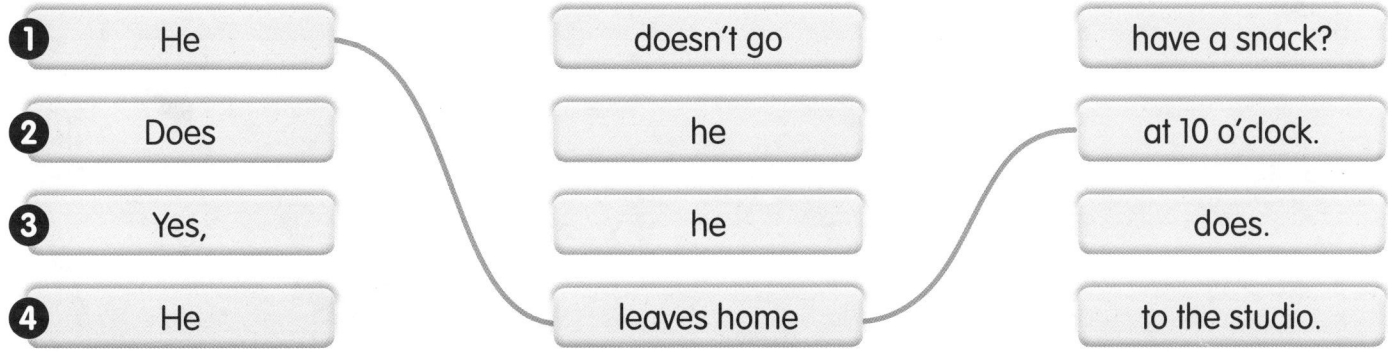

11. Look at Activity 10. Write the sentences in the dialogue. Listen and check.

Charlie: Do you want to know about my favourite singer?

Olga: Yes, please!

Charlie: (1) He _____ ,

but (2) _____ .

He goes for a walk.

Olga: Does he meet friends?

Charlie: (3) _____ .

Olga: (4) _____ ?

Charlie: No, he doesn't. He comes back home at 2 o'clock for lunch.

12. Draw your friends. Write about what they do.

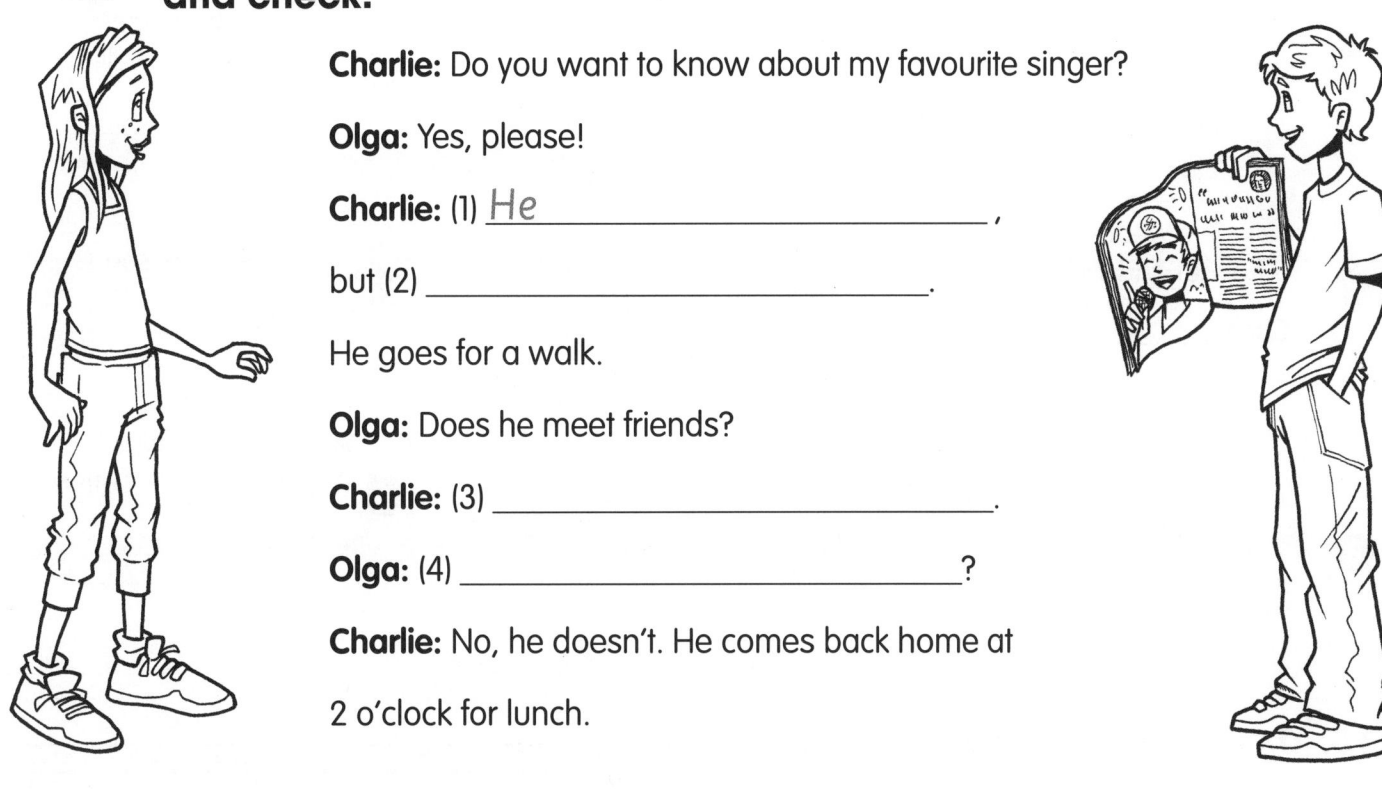

✂ **Do the activity on page 75.**

Lesson 5

13. Listen and number.

14. Read and match. Complete the sentences.

1. He is on TV. He's __an actor__.
2. She wears a helmet and jacket. She's _____.
3. He talks on the phone. He's _____.
4. She helps you get well. She's _____.
5. He sings songs. He's _____.
6. She helps animals get better. She's _____.

15. Draw and write about a job.

This is _____

_____

_____

_____

Now do the Grammar section of your diary.

Lesson 6

CLIL Social Science 6

16. 🎧 **Look at page 42 in the Pupil's Book and complete. Listen and check.**

> sports events   Maths and Science   underwater training
> fly a plane   create the rules   computer games   athletes

① Astronauts know how to _____.

② They study _____.

③ They prepare for missions in _____ tanks.

④ He and his team design _____.

⑤ They think of a story and _____ of the game.

⑥ She writes about _____.

⑦ She interviews _____.

17. Read. Write about an unusual job.

- Freddie
- mounted police officer
- train with his horse
- patrol public events
- go to horse shows

- Sandra
- tour guide
- work on London buses
- talk to tourists about London
- speak English, Spanish and French

<u>Freddie is a mounted police</u>
<u>officer. He trains with his horse.</u>
<u>He patrols public events and he</u>
<u>goes to horse shows.</u>
<u>by Olga</u>

_____
_____
_____
_____
_____

Revision: Lessons 7 and 8

1. Write the words. Listen and check.

1. _nurse_   2. _____   3. _____   4. _____   5. _____   6. _____

2. Read and match.

1. He talks on the phone.
2. She goes for a walk.
3. He has a snack.
4. He leaves home at nine o'clock.
5. She meets friends.
6. She comes back home at three o'clock.
7. He goes to a friend's house.
8. She goes to school.

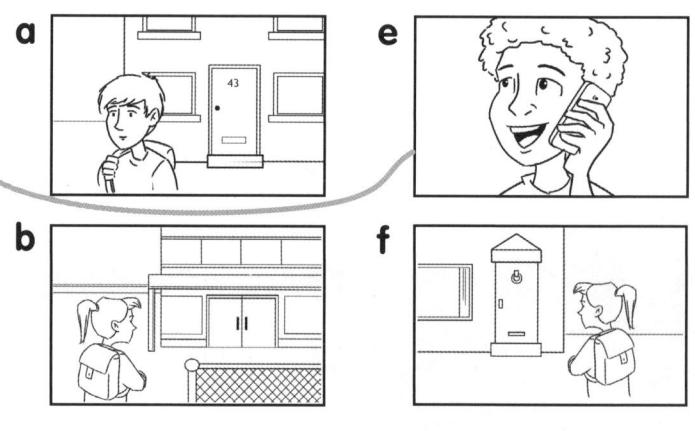

3. Write about a friend's day.

_____
_____
_____

Now do the Writing section of your diary.

Unit 7 The Castle

Lesson 1

1. Look and circle the correct words.

1. There's a **fridge** / **cooker**.
2. There's a **toilet** / **shower**.
3. There are some **armchairs** / **sofas**.
4. There's a **fridge** / **cooker**.
5. There's a **sofa** / **armchair**.
6. There's a **cupboard** / **desk**.
7. There are some **cupboards** / **desks**.
8. There's a **fireplace** / **fridge**.
9. There's a **toilet** / **shower**.
10. There are some **bookcases** / **cupboards**.

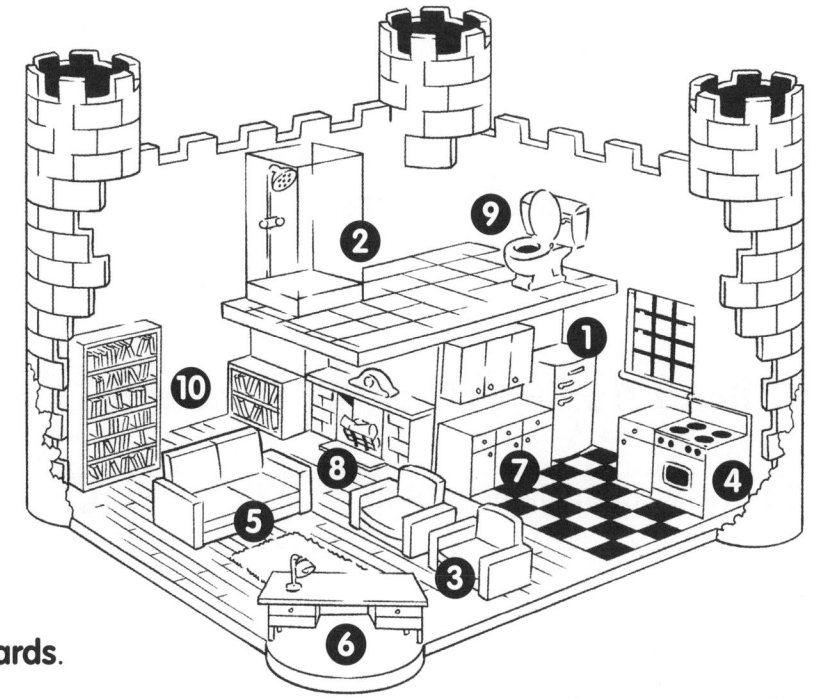

2. Look and complete.

1. There is a ___cooker___.
2. There are some _____.
3. _____
4. _____
5. _____
6. _____
7. _____
8. _____

Lesson 2

3. Remember the story: *The ghost in the castle.* **Look and match. Number. Complete the sentences.**

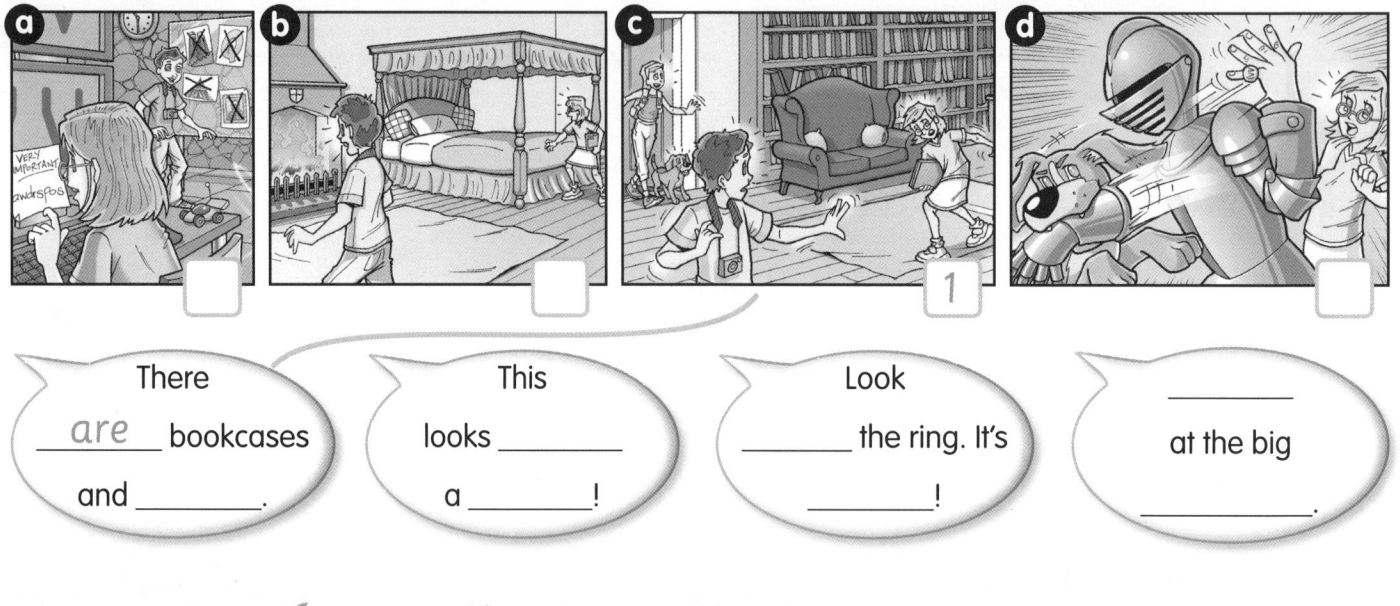

There _are_ bookcases and _____.

This looks _____ a _____!

Look _____ the ring. It's _____!

_____ at the big _____.

4. Read. True ✓ or false ✗? Correct the false sentences.

1. The children are at a castle. ✓

   _____

2. There is a ghost. ☐

   _____

3. Anna is scared. ☐

   _____

4. Max is the ghost. ☐

   _____

5. There are computers in the secret room. ☐

   _____

6. Victor Virus' next target is the Town Hall. ☐

   _____

5. Write the Quest letter. ___

6. 🔘 **Circle, sort and write. Listen and check.**

Carla

armchair

Lesson 3 — Let's investigate grammar!

The castle 7

7. Write the words in order. Colour the boxes using the colour code from the Pupil's Book.

1. a sofa? / there / Is — Is _____

2. is / a fireplace. / There — _____

3. some bookcases. / There / are — _____

4. isn't / There / an armchair. — _____

8. Listen. Tick ✓ or cross ✗.

	Anna's room	Olga's room
desk	✓	✓
armchair		
sofa		
fireplace		
bookcase		
cupboard		
It's number ...		

9. Look at Activity 8. Write about Olga's room.

1. There's _____.
2. _____
3. _____
4. _____
5. _____
6. _____

49

Lesson 4

10. Match to make sentences.

❶ Are there	are	armchairs?
❷ No,	there	some cupboards.
❸ Is	there	isn't.
❹ There	any	a cooker?

11. 🎵 **Look at Activity 10. Write the sentences in the dialogue. Listen and check.**

Charlie: Look! Here's my kitchen.

Anna: (1) Are _____?

Charlie: No, there aren't.

Anna: Is there a sofa?

Charlie: (2) _____.

Anna: (3) _____?

Charlie: Yes, there is. And there's a fridge.

Anna: What other furniture is there?

Charlie: (4) _____.

12. Draw a room. Write sentences.

_____
_____
_____
_____
_____

✂ **Do the activity on page 77.**

Lesson 5

The Castle 7

13. Write the words.

1. _fifth floor_
2. _____
3. _____
4. _____
5. _____
6. _____

14. Look and complete the sentences.

1. Where do you _____?
2. I live on the _____ _____.
3. I live _____ _____.
4. _____
5. _____
6. _____

15. Draw yourself and five friends. Complete the sentences.

1. I live on the _____.
2. _____ lives _____.
3. _____
4. _____
5. _____
6. _____

Now do the Grammar section of your diary.

Lesson 6

16. **Look at page 50 in the Pupil's Book and circle. Listen and check.**

① This is Warwick castle in the UK. It is **an old** / **a new** castle.

② The Great Hall is on the **first** / **ground** floor.

③ Guy's Tower is 39 metres **high** / **long**.

④ It has got **13** / **12** sides.

⑤ This is the Queen Anne **bedroom** / **bathroom**.

⑥ There is a four-poster **desk** / **bed**.

17. Read. Write about an amazing castle.

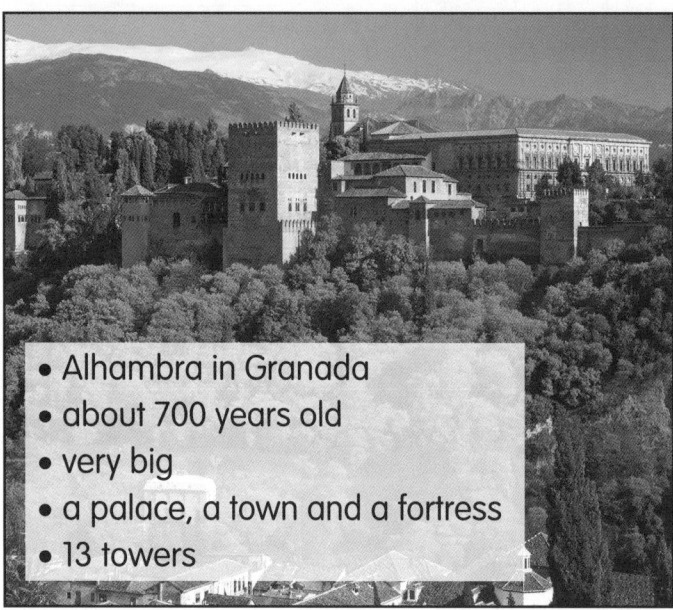

- Alhambra in Granada
- about 700 years old
- very big
- a palace, a town and a fortress
- 13 towers

- Windsor Castle in the UK
- nearly 1000 years old
- very big
- a palace, a town and a fortress
- three towers

This is the Alhambra in Granada. It's about 700 years old! It's very big. It's a palace, a town and a fortress. There are 13 towers.
by Olga

Revision: Lessons 7 and 8

The Castle 7

1. 🎧 **Listen and colour.**

① ② ③ ④ ⑤

2. Read. True ✓ or false ✗ ?

① There is a fireplace. ☐
② There are some armchairs. ☐
③ There are some bookcases. ☐

⑥ There isn't a fridge. ☐
⑦ There are some cupboards. ☐
⑧ There isn't a cooker. ☐

④ There isn't a toilet. ☐
⑤ There is a shower. ☐

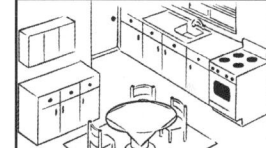

3. Look at the pictures in Activity 2. Correct the sentences.

_____
_____
_____
_____

 Good    Very good    Excellent

Now do the Writing section of your diary.

Unit 8 Science Museum

Lesson 1

1. Look and write the words.

1. He's using a ___laptop___.
2. She's using a _____.
3. He's using a _____.
4. She's using a _____.
5. He's got a _____.
6. They're writing _____.
7. She's using an _____.
8. They're using a _____.

2. Look and write sentences.

1. Anna is using an ___MP3 player___.
2. She's got a _____.
3. Charlie is writing an _____.
4. He's got a _____.
5. Olga is using a _____ and a _____.
6. They haven't got a _____ console.
7. They aren't using a _____ player.

Lesson 2 — Science Museum 8

3. Remember the story: *Stop the virus!* **Look and match. Number. Complete the sentences.**

Enter ____! ____!

What an excellent ____!

Look ____ the ____!

I _have_ to crack the ____.

4. Read and circle the correct words.

The children go to the (1) **Science** / **History** Museum to look for Victor Virus, but there are lots of people there. So Olga and (2) **Charlie** / **Anna** show a picture of Victor Virus to the people, but they don't know him. Then Olga sees Victor Virus on a (3) **poster** / **screen** and Anna finally gets the (4) **number** / **code** to stop the virus. The children find (5) **Victor Virus** / **Mr Fraser** and the security guards take him to prison. The (6) **books** / **computers** are safe and the children are very happy.

5. Write the Quest letter. ___

Write the secret word. ____ ____ ____ ____ ____ ____ ____ ____

6. Circle, sort and write. Listen and check.

pineapplessingerfishchipspiestinyTimdinner

singer
____
____
____

pineapples
____
____

Lesson 3 **Let's investigate grammar!**

7. Write the words in order. Colour the boxes using the colour code from the Pupil's Book.

1. writing / they / Are / emails? — Are _____
2. using / They're / laptops. — _____
3. are / What / doing? / they — _____
4. aren't / using / They / a games console. — _____

8. Listen. Tick ✓ or cross ✗.

Max	watch a film on the DVD player ✓	use a digital camera	
Anna and Olga	use laptops	write emails	
Mr Fraser	has got an MP3 player	has got a mobile phone	
Charlie	use a games console	use a printer	

9. Look at Activity 8. Complete the sentences.

1. Max is _watching a film on the DVD player_.
2. He isn't _____.
3. Anna and Olga are _____.
4. They _____.
5. Mr Fraser has _____.
6. _____
7. _____
8. _____

Lesson 4

Science Museum 8

10. Match to make sentences.

1. They're — they — a games console.
2. They — using — emails.
3. Yes, — they — using laptops?
4. Are — aren't writing — are.

11. Look at Activity 10. Write the sentences in the dialogue. Listen and check.

Anna: Look at the children in their classroom.

Olga: It looks fun. What are they doing?

Anna: (1) <u>They're</u> _____.

They are playing *Word Quest*!

Olga: Fantastic! What are the other children doing? (2) _____?

Anna: (3) _____,

but (4) _____.

They are watching the *Quest* DVD.

12. Look at the picture in Activity 11. Write sentences.

1. <u>Sarah</u> _____.
2. <u>Nina and Billy</u> _____.
3. _____
4. _____

✂ **Do the activity on page 79.**

Lesson 5

13.  **Listen and number.**

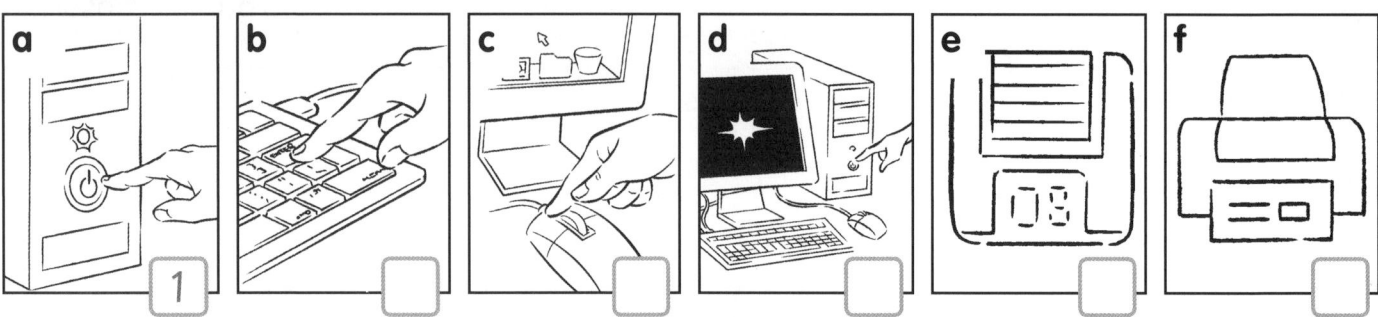

14. Read and circle the instructions for an MP3 player.

RE: Instructions for MP3 player

Hi Olga,

Here are the instructions for an MP3 player.

First, (1) **switch on / switch off** the MP3 player. (2) **Click on / Save** 'play'.

Listen to your music! Finally, (3) **switch on / switch off** the MP3 player.

Write soon with your news!

Anna

15. Look and complete the email to your friend.

switch off   enter   print
clicking on   save   ~~switch on~~

RE: Instructions for computer and printer

Hi,

Thanks for your email. Here are the instructions for your computer and printer. First, (1) _switch on_ the computer and printer. Next, (2) _____ the password. Type the information into the document. Then (3) _____ the document by (4) _____ the save icon. Then (5) _____ the document by clicking on the printer icon. Finally, (6) _____ your computer and printer.

Write soon with your news!

_____

Now do the Grammar section of your diary.

Lesson 6

16. Look at page 56 in the Pupil's Book and complete.

> solar panels   ~~robot vacuum cleaner~~   the park   different brushes
> battery   move by itself   draws energy   solar powered bag

❶ This is a smart _robot vacuum cleaner_ .

❷ It can _____.

❸ It has got _____ to clean under the furniture.

❹ You can charge its _____.

❺ This is a _____.

❻ It is covered in _____.

❼ It _____ from the sun.

❽ You can take it with you to _____ and shops.

17. Read. Draw and write about your invention.

- KK Gregory
- Wristies®
- type of glove
- cold weather

This is KK Gregory. Her invention is called Wristies. They are a type of glove without fingers. You can wear them under your coat in cold weather.
by Charlie

Revision: Lessons 7 and 8

1. Match. Listen and check.

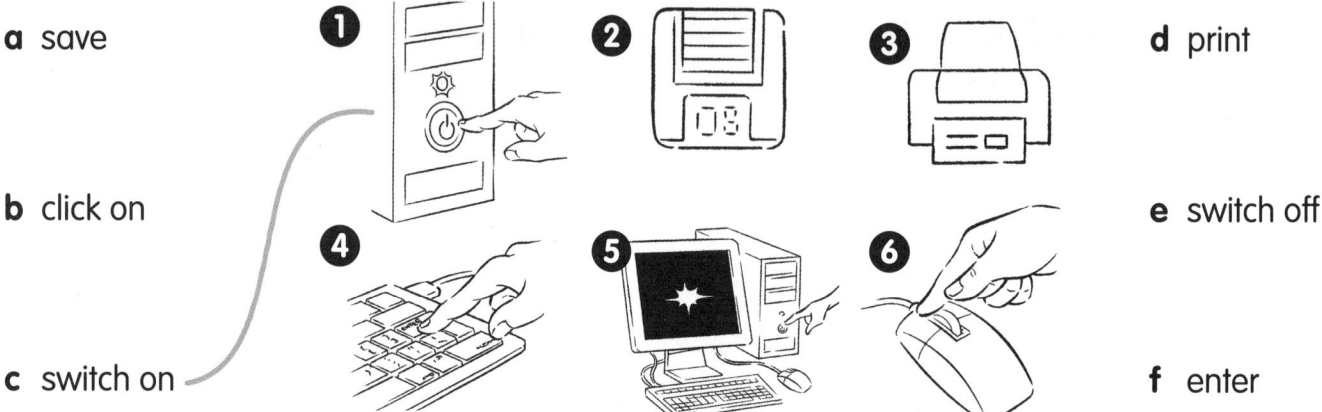

a save
b click on
c switch on
d print
e switch off
f enter

2. Read and circle.

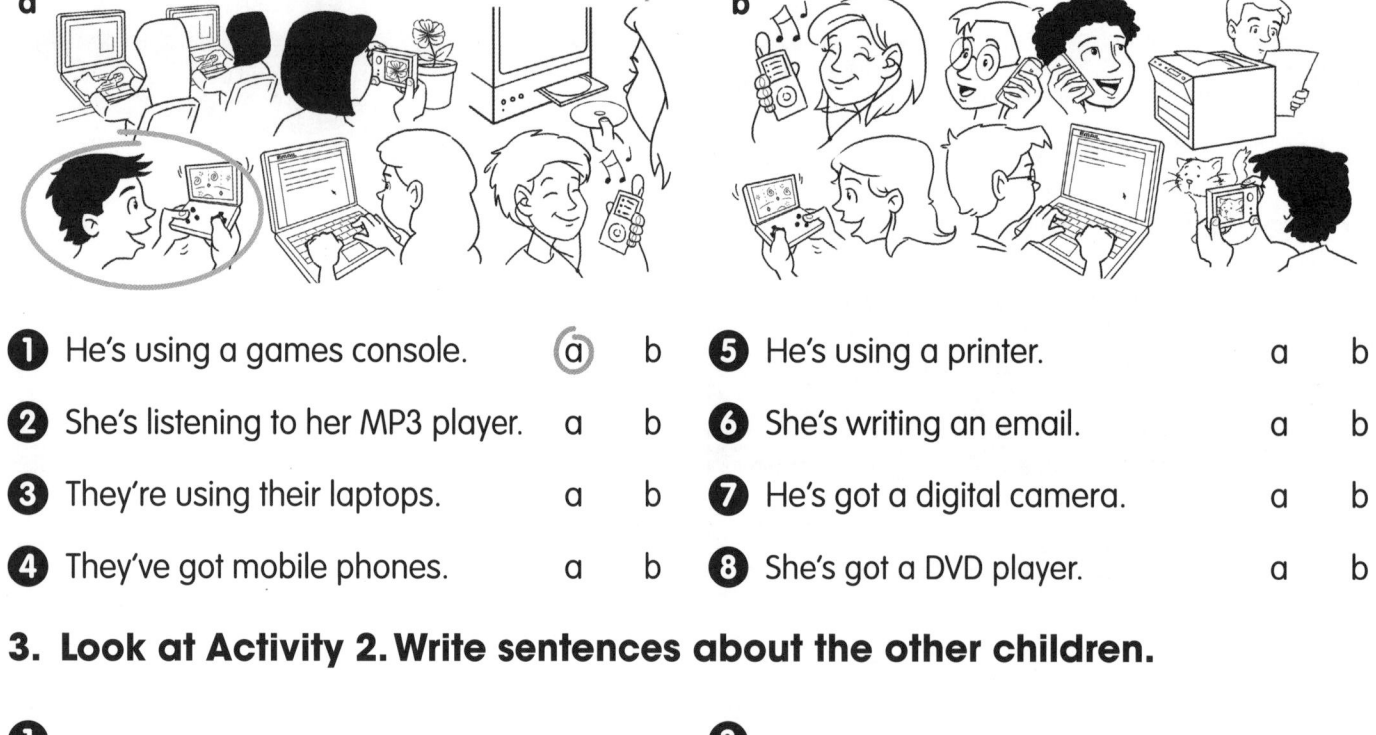

1 He's using a games console.   (a)   b
2 She's listening to her MP3 player.   a   b
3 They're using their laptops.   a   b
4 They've got mobile phones.   a   b
5 He's using a printer.   a   b
6 She's writing an email.   a   b
7 He's got a digital camera.   a   b
8 She's got a DVD player.   a   b

3. Look at Activity 2. Write sentences about the other children.

1 _____
2 _____
3 _____
4 _____

Good   Very good   Excellent

Now do the Writing section of your diary.

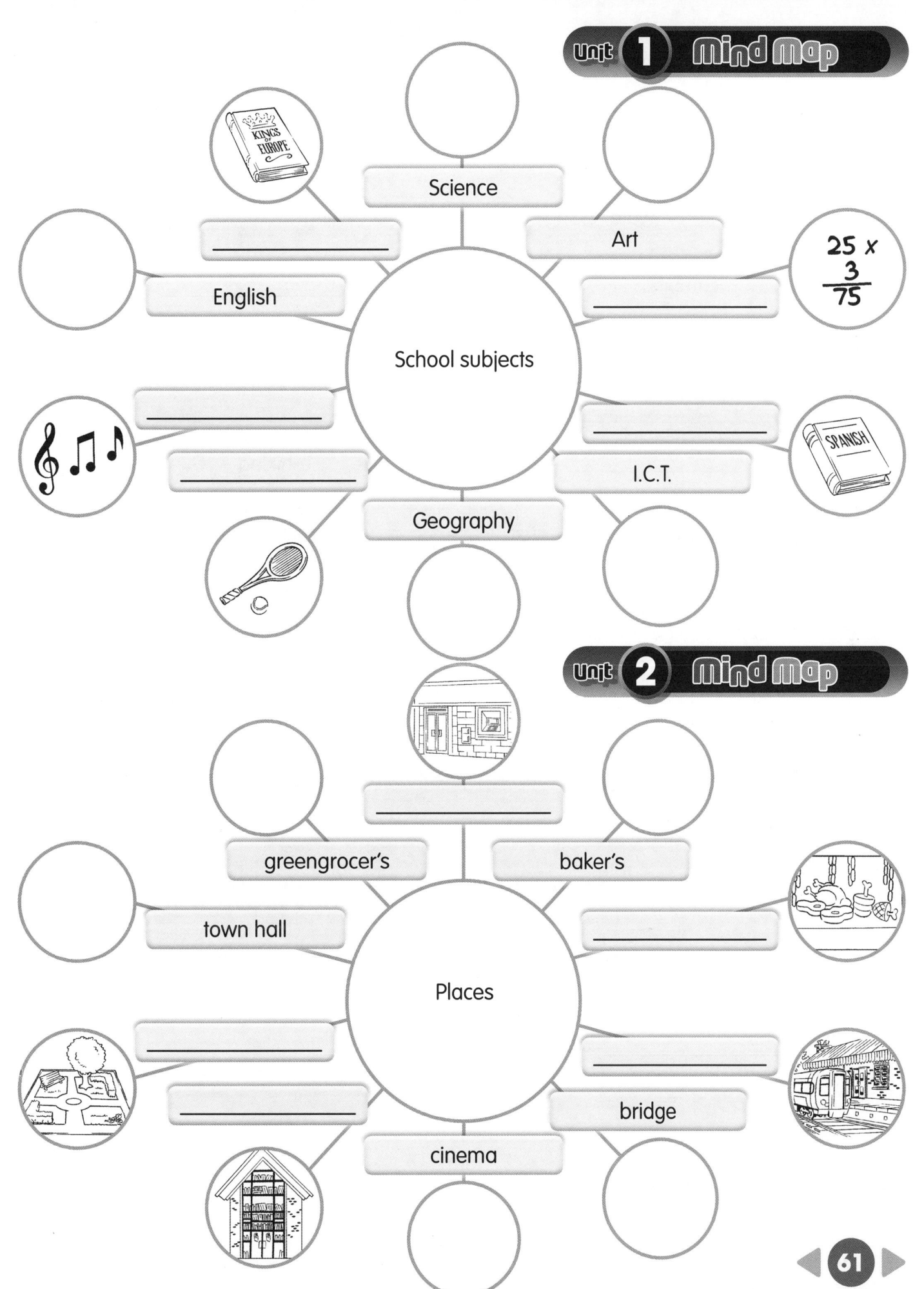

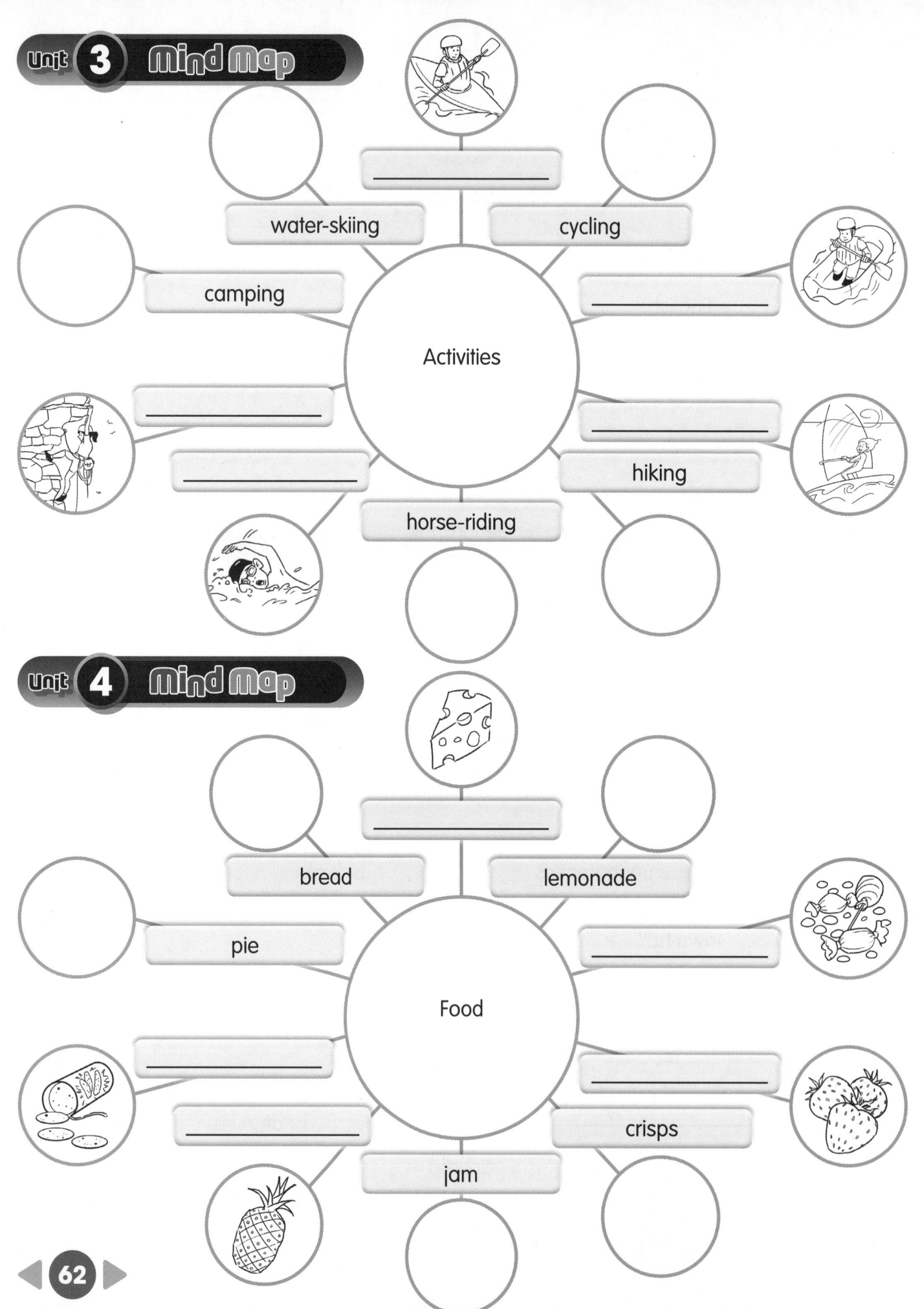

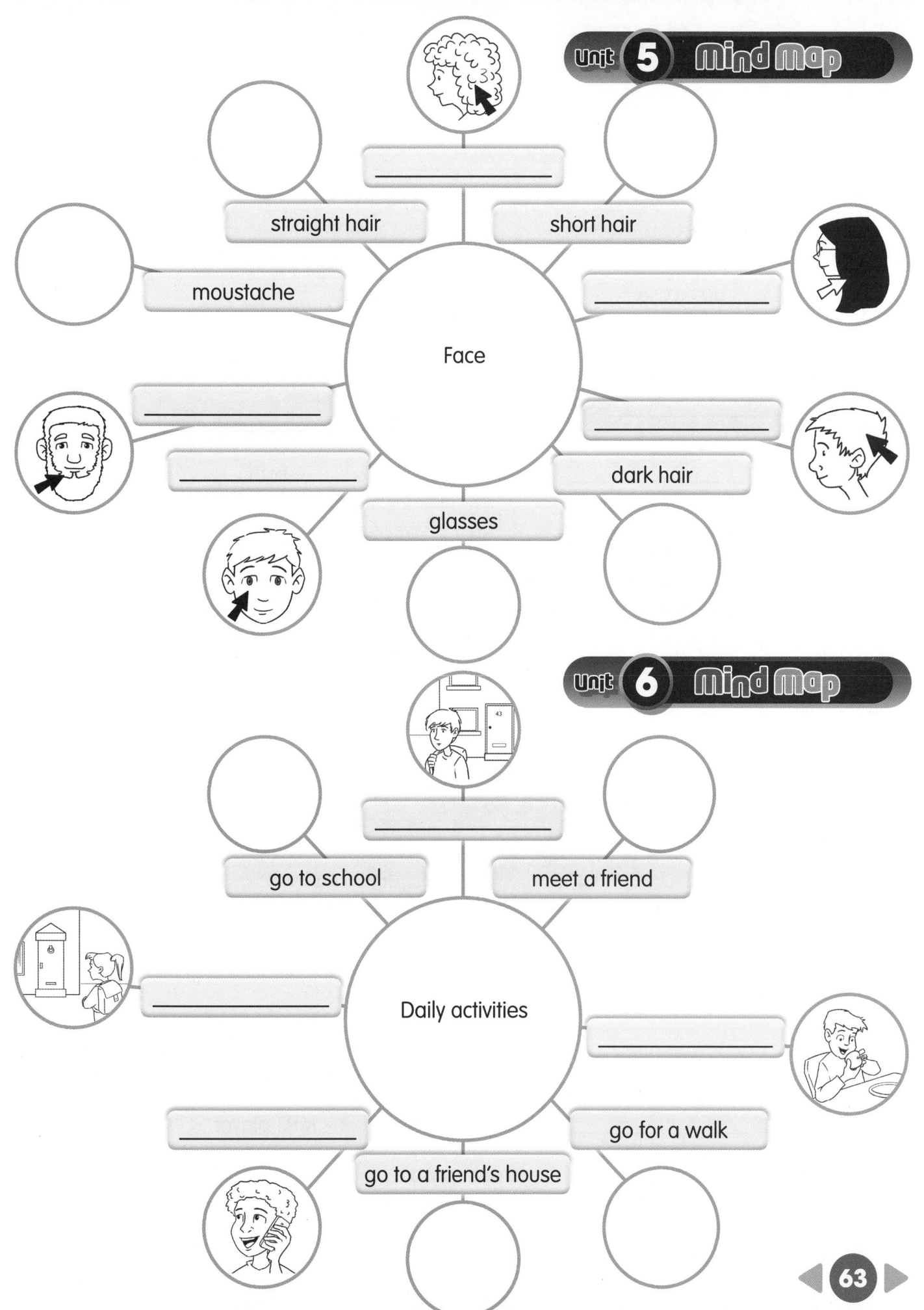

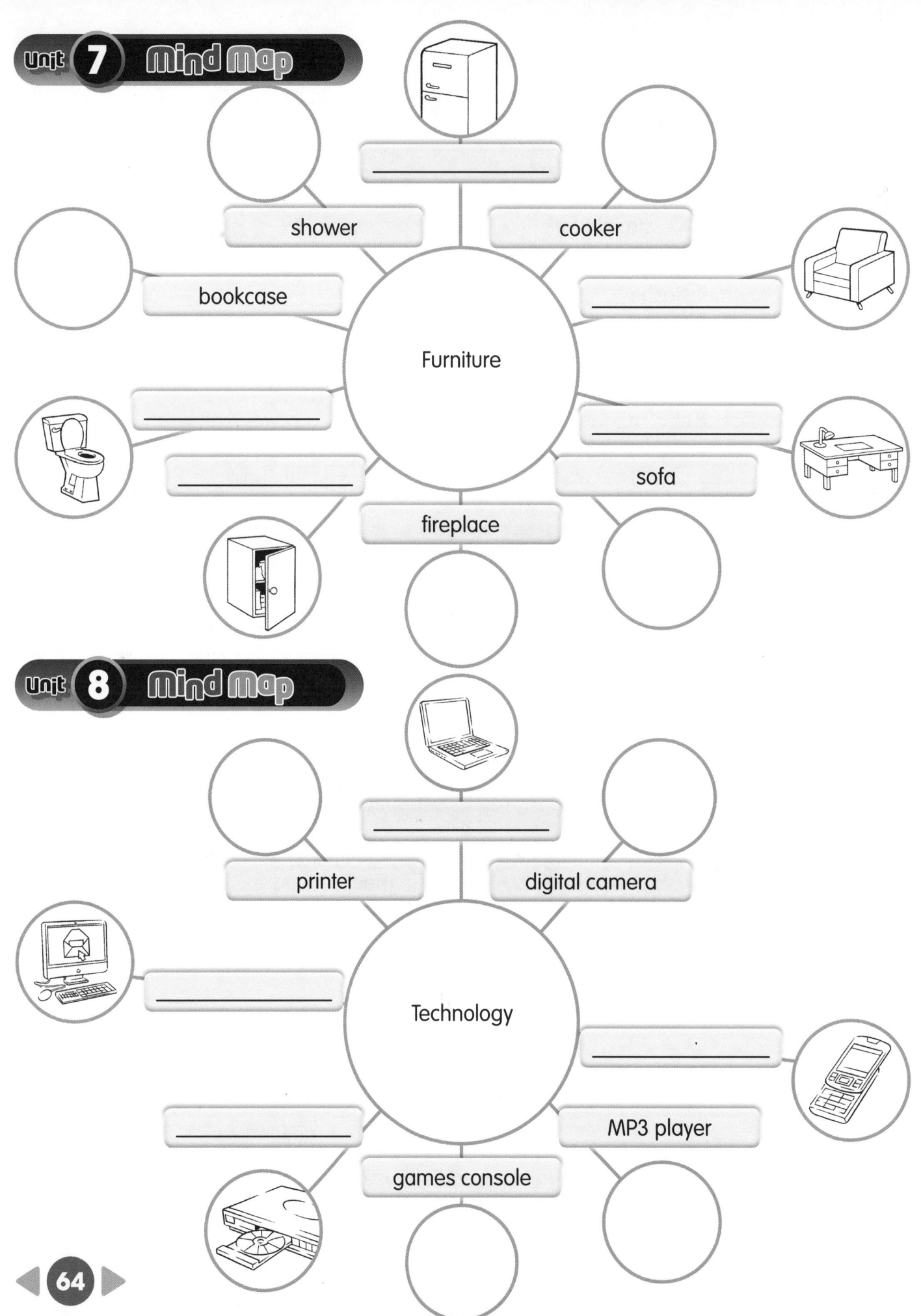

Unit 1 Guess the subject

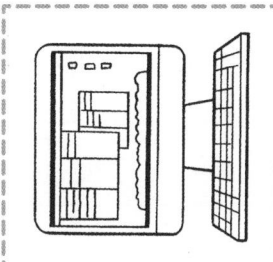
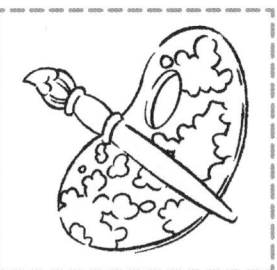

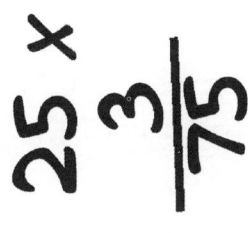
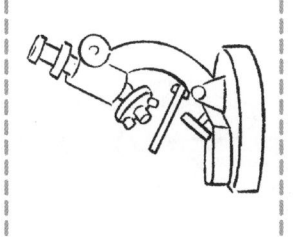

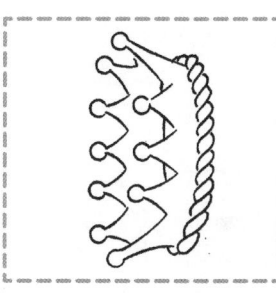

Monday	Tuesday	Wednesday	Thursday	Friday

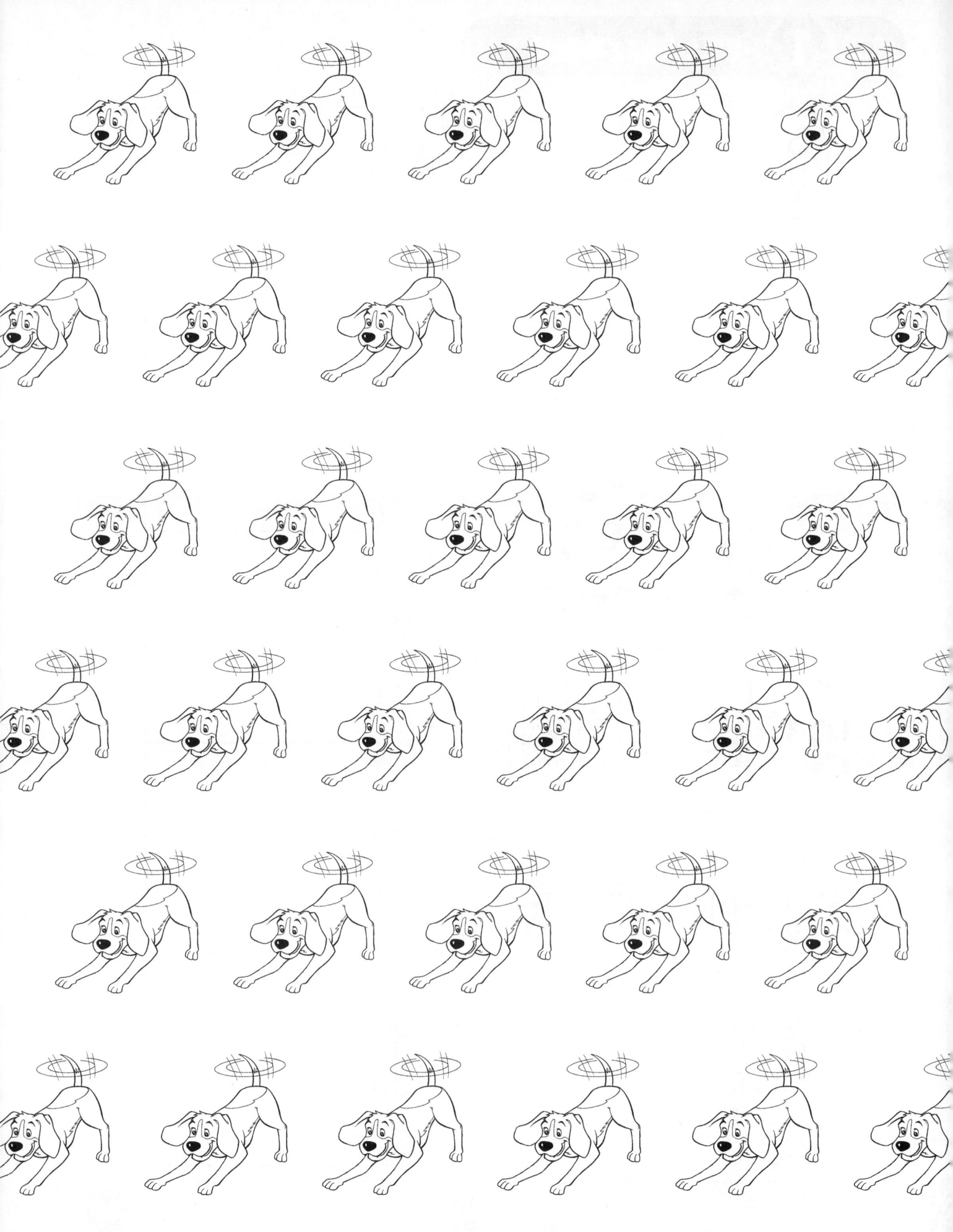

Unit 2 Place pelmanism

67

Unit 3 Spot the difference

Unit 4 Shops

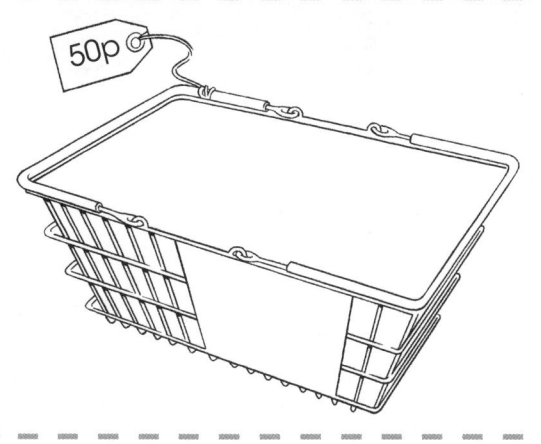

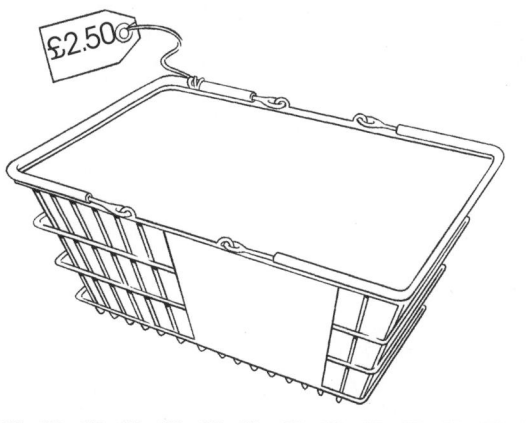

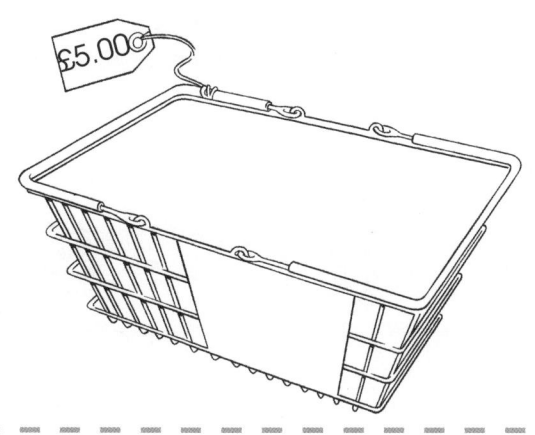

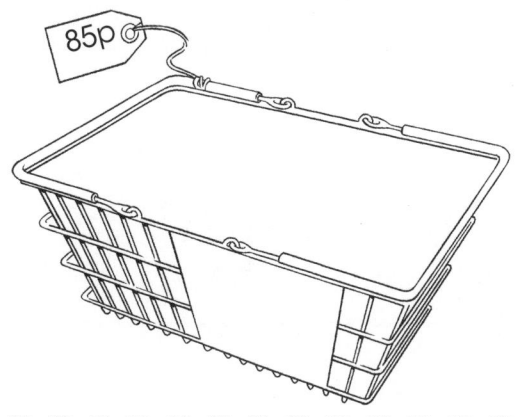

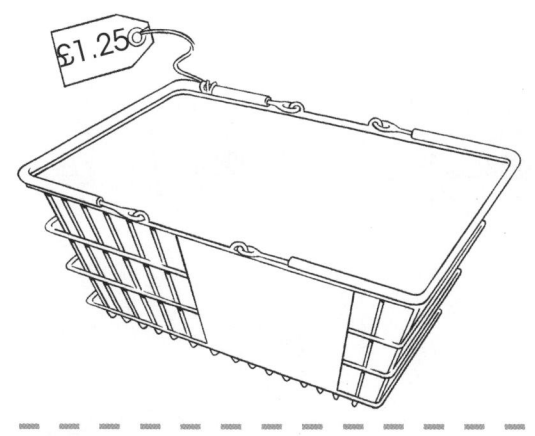

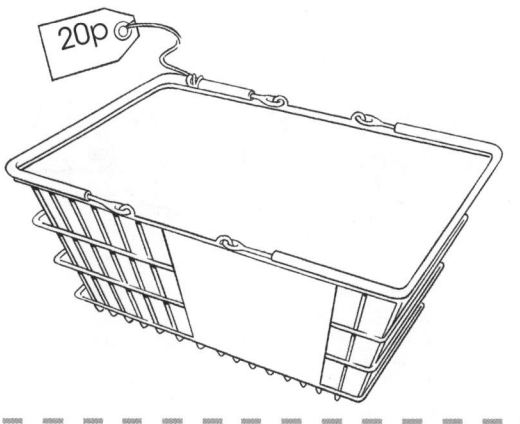

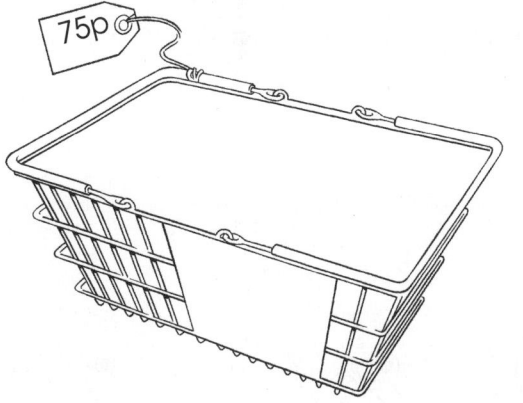

Unit 5 Create a portrait

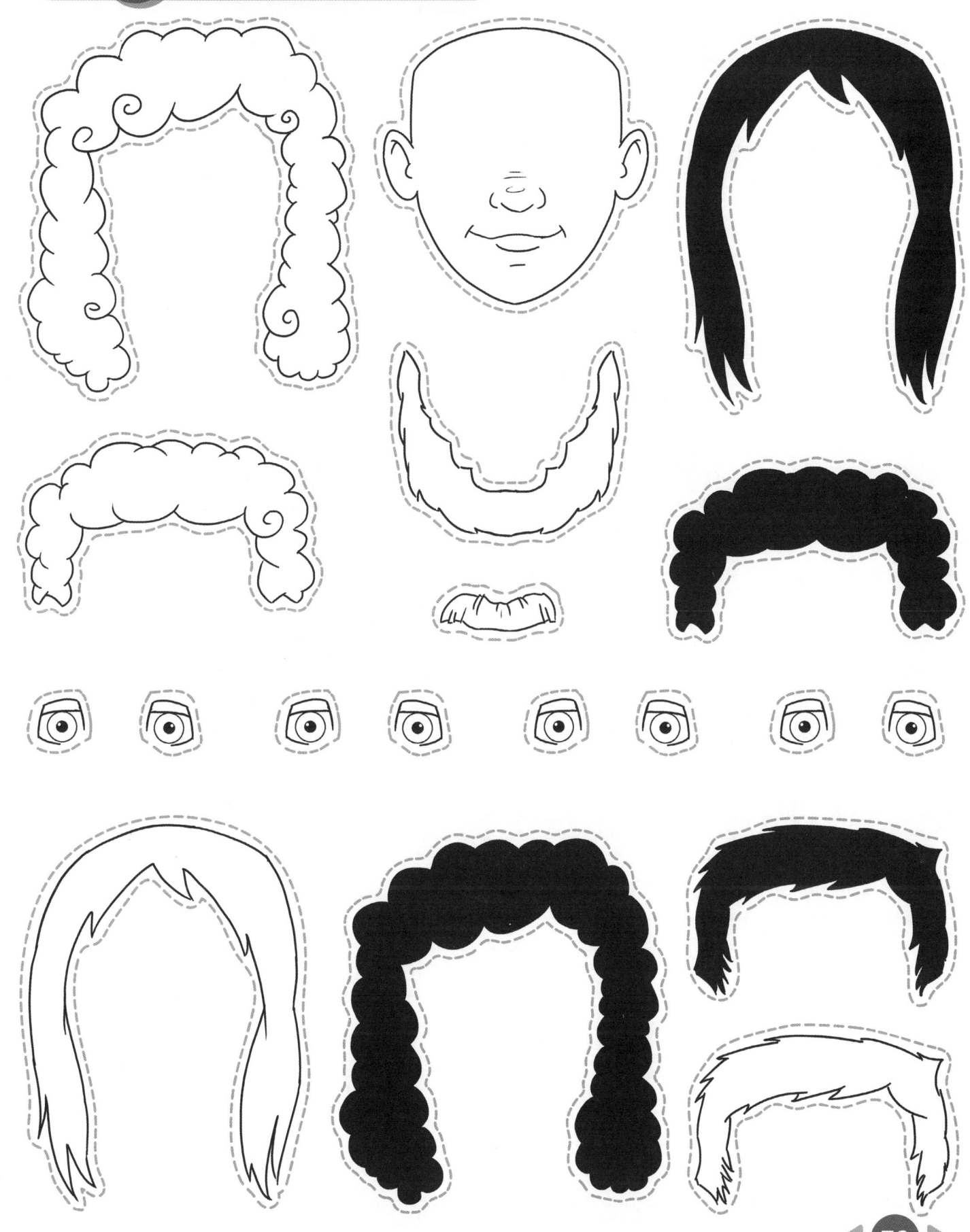

Unit 6 Tell a story

Unit 7 Play the castle game

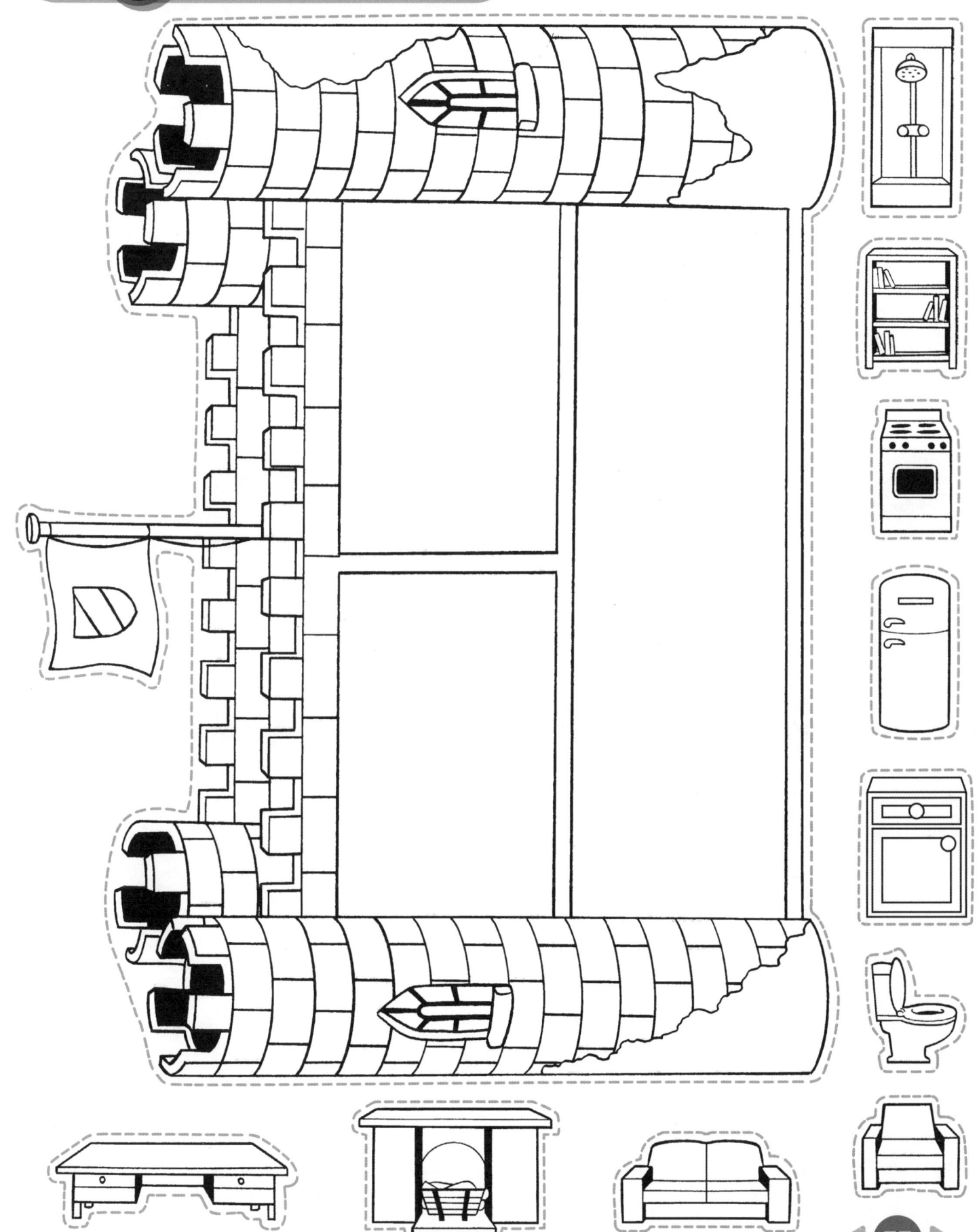

77

Unit 8 Action Snap